Lecture Notes in Computer Scie

Edited by G. Goos, J. Hartmanis, and J. van

Springer
Berlin
Heidelberg
New York
Barcelona
Hong Kong
London
Milan
Paris
Tokyo

Anni R. Coden   Eric W. Brown
Savitha Srinivasan (Eds.)

Information Retrieval Techniques for Speech Applications

Springer

Series Editors

Gerhard Goos, Karlsruhe University, Germany
Juris Hartmanis, Cornell University, NY, USA
Jan van Leeuwen, Utrecht University, The Netherlands

Volume Editors

Anni R. Coden
Eric W. Brown
IBM T.J. Watson Research Center
P.O. Box 704, Yorktown Heights, NY 10598, USA
E-mail: {anni,ewb}@us.ibm.com

Savitha Srinivasan
IBM Almaden Research Center
650 Harry Road, San Jose, CA 95120, USA
E-mail: savitha@almaden.ibm.com

Cataloging-in-Publication Data applied for

Die Deutsche Bibliothek - CIP-Einheitsaufnahme

Information retrieval techniques for speech applications / Anni R. Coden ...
(ed.). - Berlin ; Heidelberg ; New York ; Barcelona ; Hong Kong ; London ;
Milan ; Paris ; Tokyo : Springer, 2002
      (Lecture notes in computer science ; Vol. 2273)
      ISBN 3-540-43156-X

CR Subject Classification (1998):H.3, I.2.7

ISSN 0302-9743
ISBN 3-540-43156-X Springer-Verlag Berlin Heidelberg New York

Springer-Verlag Berlin Heidelberg New York
a member of BertelsmannSpringer Science+Business Media GmbH

http://www.springer.de

© Springer-Verlag Berlin Heidelberg 2002
Printed in Germany

Typesetting: Camera-ready by author, data conversion by PTP-Berlin, Stefan Sossna
Printed on acid-free paper   SPIN 10846173   06/3142   5 4 3 2 1 0

Preface

This volume is based on a workshop held on September 13, 2001 in New Orleans, LA, USA as part of the *24th Annual International ACM SIGIR Conference on Research and Development in Information Retrieval*. The title of the workshop was: "Information Retrieval Techniques for Speech Applications."

Interest in speech applications dates back a number of decades. However, it is only in the last few years that automatic speech recognition has left the confines of the basic research lab and become a viable commercial application. Speech recognition technology has now matured to the point where speech can be used to interact with automated phone systems, control computer programs, and even create memos and documents. Moving beyond computer control and dictation, speech recognition has the potential to dramatically change the way we create, capture, and store knowledge. Advances in speech recognition technology combined with ever decreasing storage costs and processors that double in power every eighteen months have set the stage for a whole new era of applications that treat speech in the same way that we currently treat text.

The goal of this workshop was to explore the technical issues involved in applying information retrieval and text analysis technologies in the new application domains enabled by automatic speech recognition. These possibilities bring with them a number of issues, questions, and problems. Speech-based user interfaces create different expectations for the end user, which in turn places different demands on the back-end systems that must interact with the user and interpret the user's commands. Speech recognition will never be perfect, so analyses applied to the resulting transcripts must be robust in the face of recognition errors. The ability to capture speech and apply speech recognition on smaller, more powerful, pervasive devices suggests that text analysis and mining technologies can be applied in new domains never before considered.

This workshop explored techniques in information retrieval and text analysis that meet the challenges in the new application domains enabled by automatic speech recognition. We posed seven questions to the contributors to focus on:

1. What new IR related applications, problems, or opportunities are created by effective, real-time speech recognition?
2. To what extent are information retrieval methods that work on perfect text applicable to imperfect speech transcripts?
3. What additional data representations from a speech engine may be exploited by applications?
4. Does domain knowledge (context/voice-id) help and can it be automatically deduced?
5. Can some of the techniques explored be beneficial in a standard IR application?
6. What constraints are imposed by real time speech applications?
7. Case studies of specific speech applications – either successful or not.

The contributions covered a wide spectrum of topics. We have grouped them into a few main categories, introduced below.

Traditional Information Retrieval Techniques

The paper by James Allan reviews the effects of speech transcription errors on traditional information retrieval tasks and shows that these effects are minimal. Allan points out that the tasks studied are based on the traditional information retrieval framework. In particular, the queries are longer than those seen in web or emerging speech applications. Furthermore, the evaluation is based on returning documents instead of paragraphs, sentences, or answers, and Allan speculates on how a different framework might change the results.

Spoken Document Pre-processing

The first area to consider is the collection itself that traditionally contained only textual documents. However, multimedia collections are becoming more prominent and one of the media is speech. Collections may contain actual speech recordings or transcripts of speech recordings and this new mixed environment poses new challenges.

Speech recordings are either translated into text (i.e., the transcript), or application tasks are performed directly on the recordings. Examining the transcripts, they are in general not perfect and tools have been developed which improve the quality of transcript. An example of a novel tool is the automatic capitalization of mono-case text. This is an important task as closed caption text, for instance, is mono-case. Furthermore, automatically generated transcripts could have the wrong capitalization and it could prove important that capitalization be uniform. Brown and Coden present a discussion of these issues and several algorithms in the paper "Capitalization Recovery for Text."

Adapting IR Techniques to Spoken Documents

Many known information retrieval tasks traditionally operate on well edited and grammatically correct text. It is an area of research to explore how these tasks operate on speech transcripts. An alternate approach is to execute the same IR tasks directly on speech recordings and compare the results both in terms of effectiveness and performance. The paper "Clustering of Imperfect Transcripts using a Novel Similarity Measure" by Ibrahimov, Sethi, and Dimitrova discusses a traditional IR task (*clustering*) on a novel domain of data (speech transcripts). Désilets, de Bruijn, and Martin explore another traditional IR task – *keyphrase extraction* – on this novel domain in the paper "Extracting Keyphrases from Spoken Audio Documents." A traditional IR task is to *segment text* and the paper "Segmenting Conversations by Topic, Initiative, and Style" by Ries explores speech features for the segmentation process. The paper "Extracting Caller Information from Voicemail" by Huang, Zweig, and Padmanabhan describes a traditional IR task (*extracting information*) in a spoken word environment. The information needed is very specific to this environment, for instance, extracting all names or all numbers would not satisfy the goal of the application.

Techniques for Multi-media Collections

To date, most tasks are performed either on a purely textual collection or solely on speech recordings or their transcripts. Tasks applied to mixed collections seem to favor textual data, which may not always be appropriate. The paper "Speech and Hand Transcribed Retrieval" by Sanderson and Shou explores this area. In particular, it explores whether one could apply traditional IR techniques with varying parameters to address the different types of data in the collection.

New Applications

So far, we have focused on traditional information retrieval tasks where the data on which these tasks are performed is speech. However, with a new domain, new tasks can be exploited. First, we must investigate whether users have different expectations when performing tasks on speech. The paper by Kim and Oard entitled "The Use of Speech Retrieval Systems: A Study Design," proposes a user study whose goal is to determine the *user expectation* in this emerging field.

The paper "Speech-Driven Text Retrieval: Using Target IR Collections for Statistical Language Model Adaptation in Speech Recognition" by Fujii, Itou, and Ishikawa addresses the issues associated with using speech as input to an information retrieval task and shows several results in this area (*integration, adaptation*).

Another aspect of user expectations that has a huge impact on all parts of an application is a "real-time" requirement. In every day life, people expect an immediate response during discourse. The work by Coden and Brown focuses on this real-time aspect and the paper "WASABI: Framework for Real-Time Speech Analysis Applications (demo)" summarizes a demonstration given at the workshop of two systems that address this issue within a comprehensive framework and architecture.

October 2001

Anni Coden
Eric Brown
Savitha Srinivasan

Organizers

Anni Coden, IBM T.J. Watson Research Center
Eric Brown, IBM T.J. Watson Research Center
Savitha Srinivasan, IBM Almaden Research Center

Program Committee

John Garofolo, NIST
Alex Hauptmann, CMU
Corinna Ng, RMIT Australia
Alan Smeaton, Dublin City University
Justin Zobel, RMIT Australia

Table of Contents

Perspectives on Information Retrieval and Speech

James Allan

Center for Intelligent Information Retrieval
Department of Computer Science
University of Massachusetts
Amherst, MA 01003 USA

Abstract. Several years of research have suggested that the accuracy of spoken document retrieval systems is not adversely affected by speech recognition errors. Even with error rates of around 40%, the effectiveness of an IR system falls less than 10%. The paper hypothesizes that this robust behavior is the result of repetition of important words in the text—meaning that losing one or two occurrences is not crippling—and the result of additional related words providing a greater context—meaning that those words will match even if the seemingly critical word is misrecognized. This hypothesis is supported by examples from TREC's SDR track, the TDT evaluation, and some work showing the impact of recognition errors on spoken queries.

1 IR and ASR

Information Retrieval (IR) research encompasses algorithms that process large amounts of unstructured or semi-structured information, though most work has been done with human-generated text. Search engines (such as those on the Web) are a highly visible outgrowth of IR research, where the problem is to present a list of documents (e.g., Web pages) that are likely to be relevant to a user's query. All of the techniques that are needed to find documents, to extract their key concepts, to recognize and avoid "spam" words, to rank the likely matches, and to elicit feedback from the user, etc., are aspects of IR.[1]

In the last several years, automatic speech recognition (ASR) systems have become commercially available. Their introduction extends the realm of IR to include not just text but also audio documents and queries. That is, a passage of speech can be processed by an ASR "speech to text" system and then traditional text-based IR techniques can be employed to help the user locate speeches of

---

[1] The field of Information Retrieval naturally includes myriad other research issues, ranging from formal modeling of the problem to engineering systems that work across languages, from document clustering to multi-document summarization, and from classification to question answering. In this paper I will focus on search engine technology, though many of the ideas and directions apply equally well to other IR research problems.

A.R. Coden, E.W. Brown, and S. Srinivasan (Eds.): IR Techniques ..., LNCS 2273, pp. 1–10, 2002.

interest—directly from the audio (rather, automatically generated text) and not from a human-generated transcript.

Unfortunately, ASR systems are imperfect. Although they do well enough to be marketed commercially, they still make large numbers of errors in the recognition process. The result is an automatically generated transcript where numerous words have been interchanged with other words that (usually) sound vaguely similar to the original. This corruption of the words is potentially a significant problem for IR systems that rely primarily on word matching to find relevant documents.

Even before ASR systems were available as commercial products, IR and ASR researchers had begun work toward exploring interactions between the two fields. The results were somewhat surprising: even tremendous numbers of speech recognition errors in a spoken document had little impact on retrieval effectiveness. Yes, there were theoretical situations where even a single error could make a system fail completely. However, those problems did not seem to crop up in experimental settings.

In the rest of this paper, I will discuss my feelings about why ASR errors have not been a major problem for IR to date. In Section 3 I will support those ideas by reviewing several research papers that explored those ideas. Then, in Section 4 I will show where IR systems begin to break down in the presence of ASR errors, allowing me to claim in Section 5 that significant and interesting open problems remain. I will conclude in Section 6 by discussing several opportunities and additional problems that may arise in the future.

2   Why ASR Is Not a Problem for IR

Why might recognition errors cause problems for information retrieval? Since IR techniques rely fundamentally on matching words and phrases in documents to corresponding items in the query, any process that corrupts the document may cause problems. Indeed, if a critical query term were corrupted in the document, there seems no chance of successful retrieval at all!

I believe this issue is something of a red herring. It is indeed a possibility, but it is not likely to be an issue often. The reason is that documents contain numerous words and it is unlikely that all of them will be corrupted—even a 50% word error rate means that at least half of the words are correct. Other occurrences of that "critical query term" may be properly recognized—and if it is a critical word in the documents, it is almost a given that it will be repeated. Further, even if by some chance all occurrences of that critical term were misrecognized, the documents include numerous other words that provide a context for that word, and their appearance is likely to compensate for the missing word (for example, the word *earthquake* might have words such as *quake*, *tremor*, and *aftershock* providing added context). This theory does, of course, require that queries include multiple words so that context is available.

The reason ASR errors are fairly easily tolerated is the same reason that word sense disambiguation is rarely a problem in information retrieval. There is an idea that one way to improve the effectiveness of IR systems is to develop a technique for automatically disambiguating the user's query: does *bank* refer to money or rivers, does *fly* refer to airplanes, insects, or trousers? In theory, if a system could automatically figure out the sense of the word intended by the user, retrieval false alarms could be reduced. [11]

However, an ambiguous query word can be made clear by the addition of one or two additional words just as easily: *bank loan, river bank, fly a plane*, or *buzzing fly*. In all those cases a single additional content word means that the problem of an ambiguous query has essentially been removed.

Now consider what would happen if that single word were surrounded by an entire document that talked about the same topic. A document that talks about flying a plane will include various forms of the root *fly*, as well as things that are flown, things one does to prepare to fly, while flying, and so on. Most documents contain a huge amount of context that support the single word, meaning that that term is much less important than it might seem initially.

To be sure, ambiguity can be a problem (the query *fly* is always ambiguous) and the corruption of that single word in an ASR document might be unre-coverable. However, in the same way that additional words can disambiguate a query, they can also prevent even moderate levels of ASR errors from dropping IR effectiveness too much.

In the next section I will briefly outline a set of experiments from TREC and TDT that support my hypothesis. In Section 4 I will show where ASR errors begin to have an impact on IR effectiveness.

3   Spoken Documents

There have been two major multi-site evaluations that explored the impact of ASR errors on document retrieval and organization. In this section, I outline TREC's and TDT's efforts in that direction, and show how their results are consistent with the hypothesis above.

3.1   TREC 1997 to 2000

From 1997 (TREC-6) through 2000 (TREC-9), the TREC evaluation workshop included a track on "spoken document retrieval" (SDR). [7,9,8,6] The purpose of the track was to explore the impact of ASR errors on document retrieval. The SDR track followed on the heels of the "confusion" track that examined the same question for errors created by OCR (optical character recognition) scanning of documents. [10]

An excellent paper by Garofolo, Auzanne, and Voorhees (2000) summarizes the first three years of the SDR track and comes to conclusions similar to mine. The summary results below are largely due to their analysis. After TREC-9 completed, the conclusion was essentially that SDR is a "solved problem" and that TREC's efforts would be better spent on more challenging problems.

In 1997 (TREC-6) the SDR track was a pilot study to explore how difficult the task would be. A small evaluation corpus of about 50 hours of speech, comprising almost 1500 stories, was along with 50 "known item" queries. That is, the queries were constructed such that there would be a *single* document known to contain the answer, and such that it was known precisely which document that was (though not by the systems). The reason for the small corpus was that in 1997, recognizing 50 hours of speech was time-consuming, and that was about the limits of technology. The reason for using known item search rather than ranked retrieval is that the former is substantially simpler to assess. The *conclusion* of TREC-6 was that ASR errors caused about a 10% drop in effectiveness (i.e., ability to find that known document at the top of the ranked list). The drop seemed to be consistent, regardless of whether the queries were deemed easy or problematic for ASR errors.

The following year, TREC-7 made the problem more challenging by switching to *ranked* retrieval where there are multiple relevant documents per query. The corpus grew to 87 hours (almost 2900 stories—still very small by IR standards) but only 23 queries were used. Most sites ran their IR systems on a range of ASR outputs, providing a window into the impact of ASR errors (word error rate) on effectiveness. The results showed a clear progressive impact from increasing ASR errors, but only a *small* drop in effectiveness (here, average precision) even when the word error rate climbed to 30–40%.

In TREC-8 (1999), the corpus was made substantially larger so that it was somewhat "reasonable" by IR standards: 550 hours, making up almost 22,000 stories. This time, 50 queries were used in the evaluation. The result: word error rate had minimal impact on average precision. In fact, the results were comparable to the TREC-7 results, even though the corpus was an order of magnitude larger.

TREC's involvement with SDR ended in 2000 with TREC-9. In that case, the corpus was the same as in the previous year, and the same number of queries were used. Again, the ASR errors had minimal impact.

Interestingly, substantially shorter queries were used for TREC-9. For example, here are two forms of the same query:

- SHORT: Name some countries which permit their citizens to commit suicide with medical assistance
- TERSE: assisted suicide

A "short" query means there is much less context within the query, so one might expect the effectiveness to drop. However, the "terse" queries were *more* effective than the "short" queries. This unlikely result may be because of how queries were constructed. In the example listed, the terse query is a phrase that is probably used commonly to describe the issue, whereas the longer query does not include the same important phrase.

Throughout the TREC SDR evaluations, even error rates of about 40% had only a modest impact on IR effectiveness. The length of the recognized speech provided enough repetition of important words, and enough related contextual words, that the IR retrieval methods could readily compensate for the ASR errors.

3.2 TDT 1998

The Topic Detection and Tracking (TDT) evaluation workshop investigates ways that broadcast news stories can be automatically organized by the events they discuss. [2] That is, all stories about the Oklahoma City bombing should be grouped together, as should stories about a particular earthquake, or a specific political rally. All TDT tasks are carried out on a stream of arriving news stories rather than on a static collection. Because the focus of the work is on broadcast news—i.e., audio streams—speech recognition has always been a key component of TDT.

Tasks in TDT include automatically segmenting the broadcast news stream into topically coherent stories, grouping all stories discussing a particular event together, identifying when a new (previously unseen) event appears in the news, and tracking an event given a handful of on-topic stories. All of these tasks were carried out using both human-generated and ASR-generated transcripts. Note that in contrast to the IR task, "queries" do not exist: most of the tasks require comparing stories to each other, meaning that a "query" is effectively an *entire* document, or even a handful of documents.

The TDT 1998 evaluation used two months worth of news from several sources, approximately 13,000 news stories.[2] The results were:

- For tracking, ASR errors had a modest impact on effectiveness, but not a substantial drop. [13]
- For clustering the stories into topics, the ASR errors had almost no impact on effectiveness.[4]
- When detecting the onset of a new event, ASR errors *did* have a substantially greater impact.[1]

It is not entirely clear why ASR errors had a larger impact on the new event detection. I suspect it is because the task itself is so difficult (effectiveness is generally poor) that ASR errors have a large impact on the ideal parameters for the approach—that is, that better and more training data may find parameters that close the gap.

For two of the TDT tasks, the ASR errors appeared to have little impact. In all three tasks, the effectiveness drop because of ASR errors was very small compared to the overall error rate of the tasks.

4   Spoken Queries

The previous section shows that document retrieval and comparison are fairly robust to ASR errors, even as high as 40% word error rate. Those results support my hypothesis that the long documents alleviate the expected problems due to "out of vocabulary" and otherwise misrecognized words.

In this section I look at the other end of the spectrum. Suppose the recognized items were much smaller—e.g., the queries rather than the documents. What, then, would be the impact of ASR errors? According to the hypothesis, the shorter duration of speech will provide less context and redundancy, and ASR errors should have a greater impact on effectiveness.

---

[2] The TREC-8 and TREC-9 corpus was created from three months of the TDT training data as well as the TDT evaluation data.

One group of researchers who investigated this problem [3] considered two experiments. In the first experiment, they recorded 35 TREC queries (topics 101-135). These were quite long queries by modern standards, ranging from 50–60 words, so one might expect that the impact of ASR would not be great. They modified their speech recognition system to produce word error rates of about 25, 33, and 50%. They found that in comparison to an accurate transcription (i.e., the original TREC query), the precision at 30 and at 500 documents dropped about 10% for up to 33% word error rate, and about 15% for the 50% rate. Interestingly, the very top of the ranked list (precision at 5 documents retrieved) saw an *improvement* of 2–4%. These drops in effectiveness are comparable to those seen when documents contained recognition errors.

The same researchers tried another set of substantially shorter queries. Here they created their own queries of three lengths: 2-4, 5-8, and 10-15 content words. The queries were controlled to ensure that there would be a reasonable number of relevant documents retrieved with the accurate transcription of the query (against a corpus of about 25,000 Boston Globe news stories). In this case, the results showed substantial drop in effectiveness, ranging from about 35% worse for 30% word error rate, to 60% worse at 50%. As the queries got slightly longer, the drop in effectiveness became less. Table 1 summarizes the results from their study.

Table 1. Comparison of precision loss for different lengths of queries and different ASR error rates.[3] Caution: ASR error rates are approximate, and the precision is calculated at 30 documents for the long queries and 15 for the rest.

	Word error rate		
	25%	33%	50%
Long (TREC,50-60)	-11%	-9%	-13%
Medium (10-15)	-34%	-41%	-53%
Short (5-8)	-32%	-39%	-57%
Terse (2-4)	-38%	-46%	-61%

These results were verified by Crestani [5] who did some deeper analysis of the long queries. He showed that the ASR degradation was uniform across a range of recall levels (rather than just at a few cutoff points). He also broke the long queries into two groups, longer and shorter than 28 words. He showed that although both groups degrade in the presence of ASR errors, the longer "long" queries are consistently more accurate than the shorter "long" queries.

Two groups have independently found that the effectiveness of IR systems degrades faster in the presence of ASR errors when the queries are recognized than when the documents are recognized. Further, once queries are less than 30 words, the degradation in effectiveness becomes even more pronounced. These results suggest that there is a minimum number of words necessary for the redundancy and context effects to overcome problems due to ASR errors.

5   Why ASR Is Still an Issue

In Section 3 IR and ASR was described as a solved problem. The previous section shows that this claim is not valid when the recognized item is the query and not the document—at least, not when the query is shorter than about 30 words. For document retrieval, long enough spans of speech can be readily handled.

However, information retrieval is not just about document retrieval. There are other problems in and around IR where ASR is still likely to be a problem. To see where those are likely to be, consider any technology that works on fairly short spans of text. Such a technology, when faced with ASR errors, is unlikely to find enough context and enough redundancy to compensate for the recognition failure. For such technologies, a *single* word incorrectly processed could theoretically have a profound impact.

What does this mean in terms of open problems related to speech within information retrieval systems? Here are several issues that crop up because of the length of the material being used:

- *Spoken questions of short duration.* As shown in Section 4, the drop in effectiveness is large for short spoken queries. How can the ASR be improved for very small snippets of speech? Is it possible for the IR system to guess that the recognition may be bad—because, for example, the query words do not make sense together? Is it just a user interface issue, where people need to be encouraged to talk longer?
- *Message-length documents.* Since short spoken items are the problem, what happens when the documents are substantially shorter? For example, voicemail messages, announcements, and so on.
- *Question answering.* Current technologies to solve the problem of question answering (returning a specific answer to a question rather than just a document) tend to focus on small passages of text that are likely to contain the answer. Finding small passages in the presence of ASR errors may be an issue—and the natural language processing needed to analyze the passages may also fail.
- *User interfaces.* Spoken documents often come grouped together (e.g., a news show with several stories) and need to be broken into segments. How can a user interface properly handle those segments, particularly when the segmentation is likely to contain errors? How can a user "skim" an audio recording to find out whether it is, indeed, relevant? It is possible to skim text, but audio must be processed linearly. Can a system provide hints to a user to help in this process?

5.1   Can ASR Systems Help ASR/IR?

To address the open problems, it seems useful to consider what information an ASR system might provide rather than just the resulting transcript. There are obvious things that an ASR system can provide to an IR system, but it is not yet clear how the IR system might use them. For example, attempts to use the word lattices or confidence values from a recognition system have yet to provide any benefit. [12] However, the following are things that might have value:

- *Word recognition probabilities.* Although these values have not yet been able to improve IR substantially, they are likely to be more useful for the tasks that focus on smaller portions of text.
- *Word recognition lattices.* Similarly, having access to alternate recognition possibilities may be helpful in tasks such as question answering.
- *Speaker identification.* Knowing the speaker, or some information about the speaker, or even just when the speaker changes, may prove useful for systems that need to identify material from a particular source.
- *Prosody.* It's not clear whether or what types of prosodic information can be reliably extracted from speech, but the "color" it provides to the text may be critical in some applications. For example, consider the value added if it were possible for a system to use prosodic information to isolate sarcasm.
- *Language models.* ASR systems generally contain a language model that provides word sequence probabilities. Some information retrieval systems also rely on language models for retrieval. It is likely that some information could be usefully shared across the two types of models.

5.2 Focusing the System

Another possibility for improving the capabilities of an IR system on spoken data is to focus its attention on a specific person or domain.

- *Voice-id.* Knowing who the speaker is would allow an IR system to bring a user-specific language or topic model to bear when processing the query. Such a model might clarify terms that would otherwise be ambiguous, providing a context for the *likely* meaning of the terms.
- *Domain knowledge.* Both ASR and IR could benefit from collection-specific models of language use: knowing that the user is querying a medical database should make it possible to do better recognition, and to handle the retrieval better. If the system is targeted to a specific task (e.g., a tourist information kiosk), it could adapt both parts of the system, too.
- *User interaction.* Recognizing how the user is interacting with the system might provide useful feedback. For example, if the user is getting annoyed (e.g., more stress in the voice), the IR system might be able to try alternative ways of processing the query, or might ask the user for clarification, and so on.

6   Opportunities and Problems

The success of spoken document retrieval allows the consideration of a much wider range of applications. In this final section, I briefly mention some of the interesting directions that research could go (by no means an exhaustive list!). In doing that, I am also highlighting the problems that ASR/IR systems currently have and that need to be surmounted.

6.1   New Possibilities

Readily available speech recognition has made some things possible that had rarely been considered before. Retrieval of spoken documents is the most obvious possibility. But a range of new applications are now available:

- Coping with very short queries;
- User interface design to encourage longer spoken queries;
- Helping a user decide of a spoken document is a match to his or her query;
- Summarizing speech;
- Adapting ASR language models to the collection being searched;
- Coping with collections that contain a mixture of ASR and clean text documents (typically the latter are more highly ranked);
- Dealing with other types of spoken documents such as dialogues, meetings, lectures, classes, etc.
- Contexts where the word error rate is well over 50%
- Text interfaces to speech-only systems (e.g., voicemail)

6.2   Has ASR/IR Helped IR?

Earlier I mentioned some ways that ASR might be able to help IR, by conveying more information from the recognition process to the IR system. The process of integrating IR and ASR has helped non-ASR retrieval as well, though in subtler ways. ASR techniques have resulted in more robust weighting schemes, in techniques that should be able to cope with misspellings, and with the idea that it makes sense to expand a *document* rather than a query.

7   Conclusion

In this paper I have claimed that for classic information retrieval tasks such as document retrieval, speech recognition errors generally are either inconsequential or can be dealt with using simple techniques. I have softened that somewhat with the acknowledgment that recognition errors are and will be an issue for any language-based technology that looks primarily at small spans of text. When there are only a few words available, there is no opportunity for repetition and context to compensate for errors.

I believe that the interesting challenges ahead for speech applications and information retrieval are suggested by a broader use of spoken documents. What does it mean to retrieve a meeting? How can IR systems cope with the misstatements, corrections, and disfluencies that are common in less formal speech? Can IR systems benefit from recognition systems that "clean up" the speech as it is transcribed—e.g., adding punctuation, etc?

Finally, and perhaps the biggest challenge, is how user interfaces can be designed to make it possible for people to sift through spoken documents as rapidly as they can pick through clean text? The inherent linearity of speech prevents rapid scanning, and current recognition error rates make it possible to retrieve accurately, but do not necessarily allow a human to get a good "gist" of a retrieved item.

References

1. J. Allan, H. Jin, M. Rajman, C. Wayne, D. Gildea, V. Lavrenko, R. Hoberman, and D. Caputo. Topic-based novelty detection: 1999 summer workshop at CLSP, final report. Available at http://www.clsp.jhu.edu/ws99/tdt, 1999.

2. James Allan, editor. *Topic Detection and Tracking: Event-based News Organization*. Kluwer Academic Publishers, 2001.

3. J. Barnett, S. Anderson, J. Broglio, M. Singh, R. Hudson, and S.W. Kuo. Experiments in spoken queries for document retrieval. In *Proceedings of Eurospeech*, volume 3, pages 1323–1326, 1997.

4. Jaime Carbonell, Yiming Yang, John Lafferty, Ralf D. Brown a nd Tom Pierce, and Xin Liu. CMU report on TDT-2: Segmentation, detection and tracking. In *Proceedings of the DARPA Broadcast News Workshop*, pages 117–120. Morgan Kauffman Publishers, 1999.

5. F. Crestani. Word recognition errors and relevance feedback in spoken query processing. In *Proceedings of the 2000 Flexible Query Answering Systems Conference*, pages 267–281, 2000.

6. J. Garofolo, J. Lard, and E. Voorhees. 2000 TREC-9 spoken document retrieval track, 2001. Powerpoint presentation at http://trec.nist.gov.

7. J. Garofolo, E. Voorhees, V. Stanford, and K. Sparck Jones. TREC-6 1997 spoken document retrieval track overview and results. In *Proceedings of TREC-6 (1997)*, pages 83–92, 1998. NIST special publication 500-240.

8. J.S. Garofolo, C.G.P. Auzanne, and E.M. Voorhees. The TREC spoken document retrieval track: A success story. In *Proceedings of TREC-8 (1999)*, 2000. NIST special publication 500-246.

9. J.S. Garofolo, E.M. Voorhees, C.G.P. Auzanne, V.M. Stanford, and B.A. Lund. 1998 TREC-7 spoken document retrieval track overview and results. In *Proceedings of TREC-7 (1998)*, pages 79–89, 1998. NIST special publication 500-242.

10. P. Kantor and E. Voorhes. Report on the TREC-5 confusion track. In *Online proceedings of TREC-5 (1996)*, pages 65–74, 1997. NIST special publication 500-238.

11. R. Krovetz. *Word Sense Disambiguation for Large Text Databases*. PhD thesis, University of Massachusetts, 1995.

12. A. Singhal, J. Choi, D. Hindle, and F. Pereira. AT&T at TREC-6: SDR track. In *Proceedings of TREC-6 (1997)*, pages 227–232, 1998. NIST special publication 500-240.

13. P. van Mulbregt, I. Carp, L. Gillick, S. Lowe, and J. Yamron. Segmentation of automatically transcribed broadcast news text. In *Proceedings of the DARPA Broadcast News Workshop*, pages 77–80. Morgan Kauffman Publishers, 1999.

Capitalization Recovery for Text

Eric W. Brown and Anni R. Coden

IBM T.J. Watson Research Center, Yorktown Heights, NY 10598
ewb@us.ibm.com, anni@us.ibm.com

Abstract. Proper capitalization in text is a useful, often mandatory characteristic. Many text processing techniques rely on proper capitalization, and people can more easily read mixed case text. Proper capitalization, however, is often absent in a number of text sources, including automatic speech recognition output and closed caption text. The value of these text sources can be greatly enhanced with proper capitalization. We describe and evaluate a series of techniques that can recover proper capitalization. Our final system is able to recover more than 88% of the capitalized words with better than 90% accuracy.

1 Introduction

Proper capitalization in text is often taken for granted. Most documents, such as newspaper articles, technical papers, and even most web pages, are properly capitalized. Capitalization makes text easier to read and provides useful clues about the semantics of the text. Many text analysis systems exploit these semantic clues to perform various text processing tasks, such as indexing, parsing, sentence boundary disambiguation, extraction of named entities (e.g., people, places, and organizations), and identification of relationships between named entities [3,10,11,14,15,16].

Recently a number of new text sources without proper capitalization have been receiving attention in the Information Retrieval community. Two of these sources are closed caption text from television broadcasts and output from automatic speech recognition (ASR) systems. Closed caption text is an extremely valuable source of information about a television broadcast, essentially enabling the application of text analysis and indexing techniques on the audio/video television program [17]. Closed caption text, however, is typically all upper case, which seriously handicaps the effectiveness of many text analysis procedures. Moreover, such text is more difficult to read when displayed on a computer monitor or printed on paper.

Automatic speech recognition has matured to the point where researchers and developers are applying the technology in a wide variety of applications, including general video indexing and analysis [6,17], broadcast news analysis [12,13], topic detection and tracking [1], and meeting capture and analysis [8, 18]. Although dictation systems built with automatic speech recognition provide limited capitalization based on dictated punctuation and a lexicon of proper names, the more interesting application of speech recognition is speaker independent continuous dictation, which can be used to create a text transcript

A.R. Coden, E.W. Brown, and S. Srinivasan (Eds.): IR Techniques ..., LNCS 2273, pp. 11–22, 2002.

from any audio speech source. Systems that support this task typically provide SNOR (Speech Normalized Orthographic Representation) output, which is all upper case.

The ability to recover capitalization in case-deficient text, therefore, is quite valuable and worthy of investigation. Restoring proper capitalization to closed caption text and ASR output not only improves its readability, it also enables the host of text processing tasks mentioned previously. Even in domains where capitalization is normally given, a system that recovers proper capitalization can be used to validate that correct case has been used. Although some capitalization rules exist, most are merely conventions. Our system can be used to apply uniform capitalization rules to a corpus. Such a capability is clearly useful in any system involving text input from humans, such as word processors, email systems, instant messaging systems, and Telecommunications Devices for the Deaf (TDD's).

Towards that end, we present a system that can recover capitalization in case deficient text. Our approach involves a series of processing steps that include the application of heuristics, statistical analysis, and dictionary lookup. Experiments show that our system is able to recover more than 88% of the capitalized words with better than 90% accuracy. In the next section we describe related work in this area. In Sect. 3 we describe our approach. Section 4 contains detailed experimental results evaluating our approach, and Sect. 5 contains our conclusions.

2   Related Work

Capitalization recovery is rarely considered as a topic by itself. It is briefly discussed by Shahraray and Gibbon [17], who describe a system that automatically summarizes video programs into hypermedia documents. Their approach relies on the closed caption text from the video, which must be properly capitalized. They describe a series of text processing steps based on Bachenko et al. [2] that includes rules for capitalizing the start of sentences and abbreviations, a list of words that are always capitalized, and a statistical analysis based on training data for deciding how the rest of the words should be capitalized. Their processing is a subset of our approach, and they provide no evaluation of the effectiveness of their processing.

In applications where proper case is normally expected but not available, the typical approach is to modify the program that usually relies on case so that proper case is no longer required to complete the task. The best example of such a task is named entity extraction on ASR output. This is a core task in the DARPA sponsored Broadcast News workshops. One system that has performed especially well under these circumstances is Nymble (also called IdentiFinder^{TM}) from BBN [4,9]. Nymble is based on a Hidden Markov Model, which must be trained with labeled text. When the training data is converted to mono-case, Nymble performs nearly as well on mono-case test data as in the mixed case scenario.

Rather than modify applications to support case-deficient text or provide alternate training sets for every capitalization situation, our system allows developers to apply the original text analysis application on any text. Moreover, correctly capitalized text can benefit other applications besides named entity extraction, such as parsing, sentence boundary disambiguation, indexing, and the general readability of the text.

3 Approach

Our overall approach to restoring correct capitalization in text is based on a few assumptions about the text. First, the text must have punctuation, e.g., sentence ending periods, question marks, and exclamation marks, as well as periods after abbreviations. Second, there must be a training corpus of text with correct punctuation and capitalization, and this corpus must be related to the test text (the text in which we are restoring capitalization). For example, if the test text is closed caption text from a television news broadcast, a reasonable training corpus would be newspaper articles from the same time period as the television program. Later we will consider relaxing these assumptions.

These assumptions suggest a number of processing steps that can be applied individually or in combination by the capitalization system. First, the system assumes that the initial word in a document starts a new sentence and should be capitalized. Next, the system considers punctuation marks. All question marks and exclamation points are treated as sentence boundaries by the system and the next word following one of these marks is always capitalized.

Periods require a little more processing. A period may mark the end of a sentence, the end of an abbreviation, or both. For purposes of restoring proper capitalization, however, the system doesn't necessarily need to distinguish between these three cases. Many abbreviations are almost always followed by a capitalized word, namely titles (e.g., Mr., Dr., etc.) and middle initials in proper names. In these cases, the system can handle the period as if it marked the end of a sentence and capitalize the next word following the period.

The real task, then, is to identify abbreviations where the following word is not usually capitalized. This is accomplished through the use of an abbreviations dictionary, a titles list, and a small amount of heuristic processing. The abbreviations dictionary is generated automatically from the training corpus in two steps. First, all words that end with a period at least 75% of the time and precede a lower case word at least half of those times are added to the abbreviations dictionary. A word is any token separated by white space containing at least one letter. Second, all words from the *singles* dictionary (described below) that end with a period are added to the abbreviations dictionary. This procedure produced a dictionary of 156 abbreviations from 92MB of training text. The key for each entry in the abbreviations dictionary is the lowercase version of the abbreviation (with periods), and the value is the properly capitalized form of the abbreviation, e.g.:

Key	Value
u.s.	U.S.
jan.	Jan.

The titles list is a manually generated list of common titles, including Dr., Gov., Mr., Mrs., Ms., Pres., Prof., Rep., Rev., and Sgt. Clearly other titles could be added to this list. Which titles to include depends on the domain of the text being processed.

The heuristic processing consists of three rules for identifying additional abbreviations that don't appear in the abbreviations dictionary or the titles file. First, if the word is a single letter followed by a period, the word is assumed to be a middle initial. Second, if the word matches the regular expression "[a-z]\.{2,}" (single letter followed by a period, repeated two or more times), the system assumes the word is an abbreviation (acronym). Third, if the word consists entirely of consonants followed by a period, the system assumes the word is an abbreviation.

Using these resources, the system processes words that end in a period using the following algorithm:

```
if the word is a title
     then it and the following word are capitalized
else if the word matches the first abbreviation rule
     then the word (single letter) is uppercased and the
     following word is capitalized
else if the word is found in the abbreviations dictionary
     then the value from the corresponding entry is
     substituted for the word and the following word is
     not capitalized
else if the word matches the second abbreviation rule
     then all of the letters in the word are capitalized
     and the following word is not capitalized
else if the word matches the third abbreviation rule
     then the following word is not capitalized
else
     the period indicates the end of a sentence and the
     following word is capitalized
```

After processing punctuation marks, the system applies one additional capitalization heuristic unrelated to abbreviations. All forms of the pronoun 'I' (i.e., I, I've, I'm, I'd, I'll) are always capitalized.

As the experimental results presented below will show, applying the techniques described thus far recovers over 36% of the capitalized words with better than 99% accuracy. To move beyond 36% coverage, the system must use more than just the punctuation cues provided in the text being capitalized.

The first technique we consider to increase the number of correctly capitalized words is the use of a capitalization frequency dictionary constructed from the training corpus. For each word in the training text that consists entirely of letters, the capitalization dictionary stores the number of times the word occurs in each of the following forms:

1. all lower case (l)
2. capitalized (c)

3. all upper case (u)
4. at the start of a sentence (m)

Items 1 through 3 can be collected in a straightforward manner from the training corpus. Unless the corpus has been annotated with sentence boundaries, item 4 must be collected by estimating sentence boundaries. We do this by applying the same punctuation, title, and abbreviation processing described above. The capitalization dictionary allows the system to estimate the probability that any given word should be capitalized. The probability that word should be capitalized is estimated as:

$$p(C_i) = \frac{c_i - m_i + u_i}{l_i + c_i - m_i + u_i} \qquad (1)$$

Now, as each word in the test text is processed, if it does not match any of the punctuation, abbreviation, or title rules, the system calculates the word's capitalization probability using the capitalization dictionary. If this probability exceeds a user specified threshold (e.g., 0.5), then the word is capitalized. Using the capitalization dictionary, the system is able to recover an additional 43% of the capitalized words, or 79% total, with an accuracy over 93%.

Since the capitalization dictionary contains information about most known common words, it may be safe to assume that any word (consisting entirely of letters) that does not appear in the capitalization dictionary is most likely a named entity and should be capitalized. Adding this assumption to the processing brings the total coverage up to 82% with an accuracy of over 92%.

At this point, the majority of the missed words that still require capitalization are words that can act as both common words and proper names, e.g., 'brown', which can be both a color and a surname. Proper capitalization of these words depends on the context in which they occur. Our approach to adding context processing to our capitalization recovery system is to create a phrase dictionary from the training corpus and incorporate the phrase dictionary into the capitalization processing.

Given that one of our original motivations for pursuing this work was to enable named entity extraction in case-deficient text using a named entity recognizer that relies on case, we use this same named entity recognizer to create the phrase dictionary. Our named entity recognizer, called Textract [7,15], identifies proper names, places, organizations, abbreviations, dates, and a number of other vocabulary items in the text. Textract also aggregates variant lexical forms of the same concept and identifies a canonical form for the concept. For example, Textract might identify the canonical form "President William Jefferson Clinton" and associate with that form the variants "President Clinton," "Bill Clinton," and "Clinton." The output from Textract is a vocabulary file containing a record for each identified concept that gives the canonical form, its variants, and frequency statistics for how often the concept occurs in the collection.

After Textract has processed the training data, the resulting vocabulary file is filtered to generate a *singles* dictionary and a *phrases* dictionary. For every concept that occurs in at least three documents, all of the multi-word variants (including the canonical form) with capitalized words are added to the phrases dictionary and the first word in each phrase is added to the singles dictionary as a *phrase head*. For each single word variant, if its capitalization probability (according to the capitalization dictionary described earlier) is greater than 0.5, then it is added to the singles dictionary as a *singleton*. The entry for a phrase head in the singles dictionary includes the lengths of the shortest and longest known phrases started by the word. Singletons and phrases with unusual capitalization (where "usual" capitalization means only the first letter in each word is capitalized) have preferred capitalization forms stored in their respective dictionaries.

The system uses these dictionaries as follows. For each word that does not match any of the punctuation, abbreviation, or title rules, the system looks up the word in the singles dictionary. If the word is a phrase head, $n-1$ additional words are parsed from the input text (where n is the length of the longest known phrase started by the current word) and the phrase is used to probe the phrases dictionary. If the phrase is not found, it is shortened from the end one word at a time until it is either found or the system determines that the phrase is not in the phrases dictionary. When a phrase is found, every word in the phrase is capitalized and processing continues with the next word after the phrase.

If the initial probe of the singles dictionary reveals that the current word is a singleton and not a phrase head, then the word is capitalized. In either case, if the system finds a preferred capitalization form in the singles or phrases dictionary, the system uses that form rather than the usual capitalization.

The set of singletons in the singles dictionary is similar to the set of words in the capitalization dictionary with capitalization probabilities greater than 0.5. The differences are that the singletons in the singles dictionary are initially selected by the Textract named entity extraction process, the singletons may contain punctuation (e.g., hyphens or periods), and the singletons may have preferred unusual capitalization forms.

For a final processing variant, the capitalization system can combine the singles and phrases dictionary processing with the capitalization dictionary processing. If a word is not found in the singles dictionary, the system probes the capitalization dictionary with the word. If it is found, the word is capitalized if its capitalization probability exceeds the probability threshold. If it is not found and it consists entirely of letters, it is assumed to be a proper name that did not appear in the training data and it is capitalized. Detailed results evaluating all of these techniques are presented next.

4   Experiments

To evaluate our capitalization recovery system, we used the 1998 Topic Detection and Tracking (TDT2) corpus [5]. The TDT2 corpus contains over 60,000 news stories collected from six different sources during the first six months of 1998. The sources include two newswire services (the New York Times news service (NYT) and Associated Press' *World Stream* (AP)), two radio news broadcasts (Public Radio International's *The World* (PRI) and Voice of America's English news (VOA)), and two television broadcasts (ABC's *World News Tonight* (ABC) and

CNN's *Headline News*). We used the SGML version of the stories in the corpus, which contains the original text for newswire sources and manually transcribed text for radio and television sources. It also provides markup that segments the stories into individual documents.

For our first set of experiments, we measure the system's ability to correctly capitalize manually transcribed audio, which approximates the system's performance on closed caption text. The test set consists of all of the Voice of America text, and the training set consists of all of the New York Times, Associated Press, and ABC data (the CNN and Public Radio International data is excluded from all of our experiments due to inconsistent capitalization of the documents created from those sources). Details of the training and test sets are given in Table 1.

Table 1. Data for first round of experiments.

	Training	Test
Sources	NYT, AP, ABC	VOA
Size	92.2 MB	12.4 MB
Num Docs	27,567	10,158

All of the SGML documents are pre-processed to extract just the text between the <TEXT> and </TEXT> tags, and all annotations and remaining tags are stripped from the extracted text. The original VOA documents are correctly capitalized[1], so the test set is created by lowercasing every letter in the VOA documents. Of the 1,925,123 words in VOA, 354,107 (18.39%) start with a capital letter.

Performance is measured using the contingency table shown in Fig. 1. Correctly capitalized words are counted by a, misses are counted by b, incorrectly capitalized words, or errors, are counted by c, and correctly lower cased words are counted by d. Precision is defined as $P = a/(a + c)$, recall is defined as $R = a/(a + b)$, and the F-measure is defined as the harmonic mean of precision and recall, or $F = 2RP/(R+P)$. Our scoring program marks a word as correctly capitalized only if it exactly matches the original word in the text, i.e., the case of every letter in the word must match.

We evaluate our system by starting with the simplest technique and successively adding more complex processing until we obtain the final system. The results are presented in Table 2 and the key for the runs is given in Table 3.

The first run shows what happens when the system assumes that all periods, exclamation points, and question marks end sentences. This recovers all of the "mandatory" capitalization based on sentence boundaries, but incorrectly capitalizes words following abbreviations when the abbreviation should not be followed by a capitalized word.

---

[1] The VOA documents do contain occasional capitalization and spelling errors, as might be expected from any human generated text.

System

	yes	no
Truth yes	a	b
no	c	d

Fig. 1. Capitalization contingency table.

Table 2. Results for first round of experiments.

Run	Precision	Recall	F-measure
1	.946	.341	.501
2	.996	.349	.517
3	.990	.368	.537
4	.937	.791	.858
5	.923	.823	.870
6	.946	.782	.856
7	.916	.849	.881
8	.903	.882	.892

Table 3. Description of runs.

Run	Description
1	Capitalization based solely on punctuation
2	Run 1 plus abbreviations processing
3	Run 2 plus title processing
4	Run 3 plus the capitalization dictionary
5	Run 4 plus capitalization of unknown words
6	Run 3 plus the singles dictionary
7	Run 6 plus the phrases dictionary
8	Run 7 plus capitalization of unknown words

Run 2 improves on this by using the abbreviations dictionary to distinguish periods marking abbreviations from periods marking the end of a sentence. It also allows the system to correctly capitalize the known abbreviations. Period processing improves further in Run 3, which adds title processing. The system was already correctly capitalizing words following titles in runs 1 and 2, but title processing allows the system to correctly capitalize the titles as well.

Run 4 moves beyond processing triggered by punctuation and considers every word using the capitalization dictionary and a capitalization probability threshold of 0.5, such that every word with a capitalization probability (as computed by (3)) greater than 0.5 is capitalized. This dramatically improves recall to 0.791, but causes an expected drop in precision to 0.937. In Run 5, the system assumes that any word consisting entirely of letters but not found in the capitalization dictionary is a named entity and should be capitalized. This brings recall up to 0.823 and precision down to 0.923.

In Run 6, the system uses the singles dictionary instead of the capitalization dictionary, so it is an alternate version of Run 4. Run 6 gives a slight improvement in precision and a slight reduction in recall compared to Run 4. The singles dictionary is generated by a more selective process than the capitalization dictionary, and it contains preferred spelling forms, such as all caps. Hence, we would expect Run 6 to be more accurate but provide less coverage.

Let us consider in more detail some of the errors being made by the system in Run 6. There are several types of errors to account for. First, there are errors in the original document, including incorrect capitalization (e.g., 'Madeline Albright' is not capitalized) and spelling errors (e.g., 'Phenom Pen' instead of 'Phnom Pen'). The system is penalized whenever its output fails to match exactly the original capitalized text, even if the original is incorrect, and spelling errors will cause the system to make mistakes. These types of errors could be eliminated if the corpus (both the training and the test data) was manually corrected using a fixed set of rules for capitalization and uniform spelling (e.g., some geographical locations). This is a large effort, however, and it is unlikely that these kinds of errors are obscuring a deficiency in the system that we can actually address, such that removing them would lead to a significantly improved system.

The second type of error can be described as a "context error." Depending on the context, the word may or may not be capitalized. For example, the word 'house' is in general not capitalized, but as part of the phrase 'House of Lords' it is. We address this problem in Run 7 where the phrase dictionary is added to the processing. This substantially improves recall over Run 6 with a minor penalty in precision. The reduction in precision is due in part to inconsistent capitalization of the same phrase across different documents. Since we score the system at the word level, even if the system identifies a phrase that should be capitalized, the individual words in the phrase may not be capitalized in the same way as the original.

Run 8 adds capitalization of unknown words to Run 7, similar to Run 5. This gives another boost to recall with a slight loss in precision, and produces the best results with precision at 0.903, recall at 0.882, and F-measure at 0.892.

The system's best performing run still leaves room for improvement. The remaining errors are quite challenging, however, and are due in large part to the ambiguities of the English language. There are some fixed rules for capitalization but they are not always adhered to. Furthermore, there are many practices for capitalization which are also mostly, but not always, adhered to. These two statements are apparent when looking at the statistics of words in the dictionaries. Even discounting the words which legitimately may or may not be capitalized depending on context, there are many words which have very similar likelihood of being spelled both ways, which leads us to believe that its up to the interpretation of the transcriber. Another difficult case is words that frequently appear with unusual capitalization, such as all caps. For instance, both of the spellings

'NASDAQ' and 'Nasdaq' can be found, although the former occurs more often. Correctly choosing between these two forms is very difficult.

Table 4. Data for second round of experiments.

	Training	Test
Sources	NYT-A, AP, ABC, VOA	NYT-B
Size	83.6 MB	21 MB
Num Docs	33,705	4,020

To verify that our capitalization technique works on other genres of text besides radio news transcriptions, we created a second test set from a portion of the New York Times news wire data (NYT-B, the last 4,020 articles from May and June) and a corresponding training set from the remaining New York Times news wire articles (NYT-A) and the AP, ABC, and VOA articles. The details are given in Table 4.

The results from executing the same set of runs on this data are presented in Table5. With this test set we see the same performance trends, and achieve a final performance of precision at 0.916, recall at 0.818, and F-measure at 0.864.

Table 5. Results for second round of experiments.

Run	Precision	Recall	F-measure
1	.981	.315	.477
2	.986	.320	.483
3	.986	.328	.492
4	.948	.761	.844
5	.937	.787	.855
6	.948	.716	.816
7	.936	.789	.856
8	.916	.818	.864

Finally, we explored the effectiveness of our approach in a scenario where appropriate training data is unavailable. To measure this, we used the same training set as in our first round of experiments and ran the system on a collection of Wall Street Journal articles from 1992. The test set contains 3,487 documents (10MB) and 1,531,841 words, of which 253,277 (16.5%) begin with a capital letter. The system was able to recover capitalization with precision at 0.911, recall at .788, and F-measure at 0.845, verifying that even in the absence of a proper training set, the system can perform well.

5   Conclusions

Capitalization recovery is the process of adding proper capitalization to text that is case-deficient. Although this problem has received little attention by itself, recent text analysis applications involving closed caption text and automatic speech recognition output show that there is a clear need for this functionality.

We have presented a system that applies a series of heuristic, statistical, and dictionary based processing steps to recover capitalization. Experimental results show that the system is both effective and robust across a variety of text genres and training conditions. Best performance is achieved when a suitable training corpus is available, but for most applications this is not overly burdensome, since properly capitalized text is usually readily available. Unlike other applications, such as named entity recognition or document classification, the training data does not require labeling by hand.

Our best performing runs still leave room for improvement. Further techniques to explore include local document analysis, where dictionaries and statistics are modified on a per document basis as each document is processed, allowing the system to account for the occurrence of named entities that alter capitalization probabilities for the common words in those named entities. Other possibilities for improvement include the application of richer statistical models, such as Hidden Markov Models, that can incorporate additional features (e.g., context) into the capitalization probability calculation.

References

[1] J. Allan, J. Carbonell, G. Doddington, J. Yamron, and Y. Yang. Topic detection and tracking pilot study: Final report. In *Proc. of the 1998 DARPA Broadcast News Transcription and Understanding Workshop*, pages 194–218, 1998.

[2] J. Bachenko, J. Daugherty, and E. Fitzpatrick. A parser for real-time speech synthesis of conversational texts. In *Proc. of the Third ACL Conf. on Applied Natural Language Processing*, pages 25–32, Trento, Italy, 1992.

[3] R. Baeza-Yates and B. Ribeiro-Neto. *Modern Information Retrieval*. ACM Press, New York, 1999.

[4] D. Bikel, S. Miller, R. Schwartz, and R. Weischedel. Nymble: a high-performance learning name-finder. In *Proc. of the Fifth ACL Conf. on Applied Natural Language Processing*, Washington, D.C., 1997.

[5] C. Cieri, D. Graff, M. Liberman, N. Martey, and S. Strassel. The tdt-2 text and speech corpus. In *Proc. of the 1999 DARPA Broadcast News Workshop*, Herndon, VA, 1999.

[6] A. Coden, N. Haas, and R. Mack. Multi-search of video segments indexed by time-aligned annotations of video content. Technical Report RC21444, IBM Research, 1998.

[7] IBM. Ibm intelligent miner for text. Web pages (see http://www.ibm.com/).

[8] F. Kubala, S. Colbath, D. Liu, A. Srivastava, and J. Makhoul. Integrated technologies for indexing spoken language. *Comm. of the ACM*, 43(2):48–56, Feb. 2000.

[9] F. Kubala, R. Schwartz, R. Stone, and R. Weischedel. Named entity extraction from speech. In *Proc. of the 1998 DARPA Broadcast News Transcription and Understanding Workshop*, 1998.

[10] C. D. Manning and H. Schutze. *Foundations of Statistical Natural Language Processing*. MIT Press, 1999.

[11] A. Mikheev. Document centered approach to text normalization. In *Proc. of the 23rd Inter. ACM SIGIR Conf. On Res. And Develop. in Information Retrieval*, pages 136–143, Athens, Greece, 2000.

[12] D. S. Pallett, J. G. Fiscus, J. S. Garofolo, A. Martin, and M. A. Przybocki. 1998 broadcast news benchmark test results. In *Proc. of the 1999 DARPA Broadcast News Workshop*, Herndon, VA, 1999.

[13] M. A. Przybocki, J. G. Fiscus, J. S. Garofolo, and D. S. Pallett. 1998 hub-4 information extraction evaluation. In *Proc. of the 1999 DARPA Broadcast News Workshop*, Herndon, VA, 1999.

[14] Y. Ravin and C. Leacock. *Polysemy: Theoretical and Computational Approaches*. Oxford University Press, 2000.

[15] Y. Ravin, N. Wacholder, and M. Choi. Disambiguation of names in text. In *Proc. of the Fifth ACL Conf. on Applied Natural Language Processing*, pages 202–208, Washington, D.C., 1997.

[16] J. Reynar and A. Ratnaparkhi. A maximum entropy approach to identifying sentence boundaries. In *Proc. of the Fifth ACL Conf. on Applied Natural Language Processing*, Washington, D.C., 1997.

[17] B. Shahraray and D. Gibbon. Automated authoring of hypermedia documents of video programs. In *Proc. of the Third ACM International Conf. on Multimedia*, San Francisco, 1995.

[18] A. Waibel, M. Bett, M. Finke, and R. Stiefelhagen. Meeting browser: Tracking and summarizing meetings. In *Proc. of the 1998 DARPA Broadcast News Transcription and Understanding Workshop*, 1998.

Clustering of Imperfect Transcripts Using a Novel Similarity Measure

Oktay Ibrahimov[1], Ishwar Sethi[1], and Nevenka Dimitrova[2]

[1] Intelligent Information Engineering Laboratory
Department of Computer Science and Engineering
Oakland University, Rochester, MI 48309
{ibrahimo,isethi}@oakland.edu

[2] Philips Research
345 Scarborough Road
Briarcliff Manor, NY10510-2099
nevenka.dimitrova@philips.com

Abstract. There has been a surge of interest in the last several years in methods for automatic generation of content indices for multimedia documents, particularly with respect to video and audio documents. As a result, there is much interest in methods for analyzing transcribed documents from audio and video broadcasts and telephone conversations and messages. The present paper deals with such an analysis by presenting a clustering technique to partition a set of transcribed documents into different meaningful topics. Our method determines the intersection between matching transcripts, evaluates the information contribution by each transcript, assesses the information closeness of overlapping words and calculates similarity based on Chi-square method. The main novelty of our method lies in the proposed similarity measure that is designed to withstand the imperfections of transcribed documents. Experimental results using documents of varying quality of transcription are presented to demonstrate the efficacy of the proposed methodology.

1 Introduction

The field of multimedia information retrieval has seen a phenomenal growth in the last decade. The need for methods that can automatically generate content indices for video and audio documents has brought together researchers from many disciplines including image and speech processing, machine learning and pattern recognition, natural language processing, and information retrieval. The early efforts in this field were focused mainly on analyzing images and videos. These efforts have led to a set of powerful methods for video segmentation [1, 2], key-frame extraction [3,4], camera motion characterization [5], etc. However, the experience has been that no single modality of a multimedia document alone can yield rich enough content indices to build multimedia information retrieval systems that can satisfy the needs of a broad range of users. Consequently many

A.R. Coden, E.W. Brown, and S. Srinivasan (Eds.): IR Techniques ..., LNCS 2273, pp. 23–35, 2002.

researchers have explored the use of closed captions and audio to build more useful and reliable content indices [6,7,8].

While the methods analyzing closed caption text are closely tied to video analysis, the situation in the case of audio is different. Since an audio document can exist on its own, for example the recording of a radio broadcast, or as an integral part of a multimedia document, for example the soundtrack of a video or TV news broadcast, the interest in methods for analyzing audio documents have consequently focused on two main directions. First, there are researchers who have looked at soundtracks to build indices that can complement information extracted from the picture-track of a video. Examples of work in this category include several general audio data classification schemes that have been proposed to segment an audio document into coherent chunks of different types of audio classes - music, speech, speech and music, and etc., [9,10,11,12,13]. The second group of researchers has been more interested in generating transcripts of audio documents through automatic speech recognition and their analysis for automatic indexing. An example of work of this type is the work by Coden and Brown [15] who have been investigating the use of IBM ViaVoice speech recognition software by building a special acoustic model for broadcast news with the goal of finding collateral information pertinent to a live news broadcast in real time. The efforts in this category are many more [14,23]. These have been mainly reported at TREC (Text Retrieval Conference organized annually by National Institute of Standards and Technology) under the label of Spoken Document Retrieval (SDR) [16,17,18]. These efforts have shown the possibility of applying automatic speech recognition technology to audio broadcasts to perform indexing and retrieval with a good degree of success [19]. However, the success of many of these methods depends upon the size and quality of transcription.

Our interest in the area of audio analysis spans both of the above stated directions. We are interested in analyzing audio information to supplement video information. An example of such a recent work is the person identification in TV programs work of Li et al [20] of our group where speaker identification and face detection and recognition techniques are used in a complementary manner. We are also interested in making use of automatic speech recognition technology to obtain transcripts for audio chunks that are labeled as speech chunks for further analysis and indexing. Since such transcribed chunks are expected to exhibit transcription errors, poor topic boundaries, and small size, we have been investigating methods for suitably measuring similarity between such chunks of transcribed documents. In this paper we present the results of such an investigation using a novel similarity measure based on Chi-Square test. We use the proposed measure in a clustering algorithm to segment two collections of transcribed documents. The first collection is an archive of audio news broadcasts with a good quality of transcription. The other collection is a set of transcribed documents obtained via four different models of IBM ViaVoice trained by four different speakers. The quality of a transcript in this collection correlates with the quality of corresponding speaker model and varies greatly from good to very poor. Our results show that the suggested similarity measure is robust enough to be used for poorly transcribed speech segments in multimedia applications. The organization of the rest of the paper is as follows. In section 2 we introduce a novel similarity measure between transcripts. In section 3 we discuss our document clustering algorithm. In section 4 we present the experimental results. Finally, we conclude the paper in section 5.

2 Measuring Similarity between Transcripts

In general, automatically transcribed text suffers from several additional problems not present in traditional text retrieval systems. These include transcription errors, for example the occurrence of inappropriate, erroneous words, ill-defined boundaries between different topics, and additional ambiguity or loose use of expressions inherent in conversational speech in contrast with a prepared or written speech. The fact that the same amount of information could be delivered by different sets of words contributes additional difficulty and makes the problem more complicated.

Taking into account the above set of difficulties, our approach for measuring similarity consists of the following steps:

1. **Transcript intersection:** Determine the intersection via common words between matching transcripts.
2. **Information contribution:** Evaluate the amount of information that every matching document contributes to the intersection.
3. **Informative closeness:** Assess informative closeness of overlapping words.
4. **Similarity measure:** Calculate the similarity of matching documents.

2.1 Transcript Intersection

In our approach we make an assumption that the amount of information contained in a document could be evaluated via summing the amount of information contained in the member words. Similarly, the amount of information contained in some part of a document might be evaluated via summing the amount of information contained in the corresponding words. For words, we assume that the amount of information conveyed by a word can be represented by means of the weight assigned to it. There are a number of methods that have been developed for weighting of words [21,22]. In our approach we use the Okapi technique [21], which has proved to be efficient in a number of applications [23, 24]. Thus, we will calculate the *Combined Weight* of a word by formula (1):

$$CW(w_i|D_j) = \frac{(K+1) \times CFW(w_i) \times TF(w_i, D_j)}{K \times ((1-b) + b \times NDL(D_j)) + TF(w_i, D_j)} \qquad (1)$$

where $CFW(w_i) = \log(\frac{N}{n(w_i)})$ is the collection frequency weight, N is the total number of documents and $n(w_i)$ is the number of documents containing the word w_i. The quantity $TF(w_i, D_j)$ is the frequency of word w_i in the document D_j and $NDL(D_j)$ is the length of the document D_j normalized by the mean document length. The empirically determined constant b controls the influence of document length and is equal to 0.75. Another constant K may be viewed as a discounting parameter on the word frequency: when K is 0, the combined weight reduces to the collection frequency weight; as K increases the combined weight asymptotically approaches $tf * itf$ [21]. In our case K is equal to 2.

Now, in accordance with assumptions stated above, we can easily get the weight of a document and weights of any of its parts via applying the formula (2).

$$DW(D_i) = \sum_{w_k \in D_i} CW(w_k) \tag{2}$$

To obtain common words between documents, we consider the fact that not all words in documents are equally informative. Furthermore, we take into account the rather high probability for erroneous words found in automatically transcribed documents. Thus, we first sort all words in transcripts by their weights and retain only those whose weights are greater than some preset threshold (this threshold has been determined empirically). These words are the only words considered for co-occurrence. By doing this we make a tacit assumption that there is a little chance for erroneous words to appear in a text collection in a systematic way and as a result they should get less weight and, in general, not appear in the top of the sorted words. Our assumption is based on empirical observations where we have noticed that a speech recognizer rarely makes the same error across different speakers.

2.2   Information Contribution

As the words appearing in the intersection of documents generally convey different amount of information with respect to the documents to which they belong, we estimate the amount of information conveyed by every document to be the intersection (3):

$$INTER(D_i, D_j) = \frac{DW(D_i \cap D_j)}{DW(D_i)} \tag{3}$$

It is easy to derive from (3) the following inequality, which will be generally true when $D_i \neq D_j$ (figure 1).

$$INTER(D_i, D_j) \neq INTER(D_j, D_i) \tag{4}$$

2.3   Informative Closeness

Having determined the common words, we next evaluate informative closeness of the words appearing in the intersection. This is done by representing the matching documents via their histograms (figure 2). To evaluate informative similarity

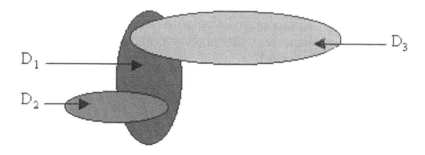

Fig. 1. Interlinks between documents D1, D2, D3

of the words belonging to the intersection in respect to matching documents, we apply Chi-square technique in a slightly reverse way. To carry out this step, we use the assumption that words w_k of the document D_i with the corresponding weights $CW(w_k|w_k \in D_i)$ constitute the set of words with the expected distribution of weights, and, the same words w_k but belonging to the document D_j with the weights $CW(w_k|w_k \in D_j)$ constitute the set of words with the observed distribution of weights. Finally, we assume that the null hypothesis, stating that two sets fit each other with some value of significance, is true. Thus, we can determine the significance value making our hypothesis true.

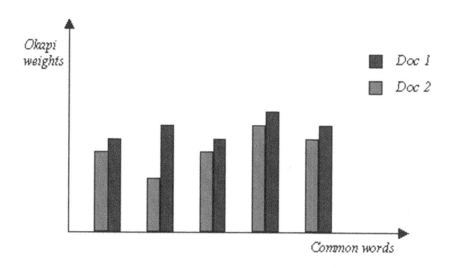

Fig. 2. Histograms of common words of two matching documents

Through calculating by formula (5) chi-square values for observed and expected sets of words, and matching the value of χ^2 with the critical values for χ^2 through the standard table, we can easily find a significance value δ that will make our null hypothesis true.

$$\chi^2 = \sum_{w_k \in D_i \cap D_j} \frac{(CW(w_k|w_k \in D_i) - CW(w_k|w_k \in D_j))^2}{CW(w_k|w_k \in D_j)} \tag{5}$$

Now having all necessary components we can calculate the similarity between two matching documents applying the formula (6):

$$sim(D_i, D_j) = \delta \times INTER(D_i, D_j) \tag{6}$$

Obviously, for (6) we have the following inequality, which will yield the value 1 if and only if $D_i = D_j$:

$$0 \leq sim(D_i, D_j) \leq 1 \tag{7}$$

3   Transcript Clustering

In order to develop content indices, one of our goals is to be able to identify topics in a stream of transcripts. To develop a database of topics in an unsupervised manner, we have explored the use of the above similarity measure in a sequential clustering procedure with the notion of "informative field" of a document. By informative field we reflect the range of information provided by a document. A cluster is, thus, a set of documents with "similar informative fields". We consider two documents D_i and D_j to be informative similar if $sim(D_i, D_j) > \tau$, where τ is some threshold. In our case $\tau = 0.15$.

The basic idea of the algorithm consists in determining of centers of distinguishing informative fields - centroids - and then finding the related documents. The centroids in our case are also documents with the condition that a document chosen as a centroid of a cluster occupies the most of the information field associated with the cluster. The main steps of the clustering algorithm are as follows:

1. Let $k = 1$ be the index of the current cluster under construction, and $i = 1$ be the index of the current document.
2. Suppose that document D_i is the centroid C_k^* of cluster k.
3. Determine all documents, which are similar to C_k^* using the similarity measure described in 2.4.
4. Among all documents D_j determined in the previous step, find the document which gives the lowest value for the following ratio:

$$D' = \min_{j}\{\frac{sim(D_i, C_k^*)}{sim(C_k^*, D_i)}\} \tag{8}$$

5. Let i^* be the index of the document D' thus found.
6. If $i \neq i^*$, assign the value of i^* to i and go to the step 2.
7. Otherwise, the centroid for the current cluster has been found. Mark all documents determined at the step 3 as members of the cluster k and increment k.
8. Find the first document that doesn't belong to any clusters determined earlier and set its index to i.
9. Go to the step 2.

4   Experimental Results

To demonstrate the performance of the suggested similarity measure and the clustering procedure, we present results of three experiments. In these experiments, we use a primary vocabulary organized as a table of basic and derived words that contains about 7K rows. Each row represents either a noun or a verb. The nouns are represented with their singular and plural forms, as well as with corresponding adjectives, whereas verbs are represented with their term forms and other derived words. The entire table contains about 30K words. Besides, we use a stop-list vocabulary that consists of the commonly used and well-known list of words, and a list of additional words supplemented by us. In our current work we have extended the stop-list vocabulary with words that represent numeric data (one, first, tens, etc.), some adjectives like "beautiful", "horrible", "terrible", etc., as well as with names of months, weekdays, and some adverbs like "definitely", "certainly", "currently" etc. In addition to above mentioned vocabularies we also use a set of auxiliary words - words that were not eliminated by the stopping stage and also not found in a primary dictionary, and a set of proper names. Words from auxiliary set are retained in post-processed (stopping and table look-up) documents as they are and are considered while exploring similarities between documents. Storing proper names in a special set is based on the consideration that proper names convey significantly more information compared with ordinary words, and so on word weighting stage we increase the weights of these words by multiplying the corresponding Okapi weights with a constant.

Our first experiment was performed to see how well the similarity measure works in presence of transcription errors. In this experiment, we compute similarity between an original document, read by a native female speaker, and two other transcribed versions, also read by native female speakers. All transcripts were obtained by reading stories to an IBM ViaVoice 1998 system trained by the first speaker. Documents dealing with two types of stories, business and politics were used in the experiments. The word error rate for the transcribed documents was found to vary in the interval of 2-10%. Table 1 shows the values of the similarity measure obtained. The highest value of similarity is 0.995 because the significance value used in the chi-square test is 0.995. The first number in a cell shows the similarity between original document and current transcript whereas the second number shows the reverse similarity.

The numbers in Table 1 indicate that the suggested measure is good at capturing the similarity between documents in spite of the transcription errors. To

Table 1.

	Orig. Reader	Reader A	Reader B
Business 1	0.995 / 0.995	0.6457 / 0.6360	0.6467 / 0.5856
Business 2	0.995 / 0.995	0.7057 / 0.6546	0.6482 / 0.5584
Politics 1	0.995 / 0.995	0.8622 / 0.7295	0.8577 / 0.8162
Politics 2	0.995 / 0.995	0.7783 / 0.6514	0.7666 / 0.6838

further show that the measure is good at discriminating between different types of documents, we show in Table 2 the pair-wise similarities between the original versions of the four documents of Table 1.

Table 2.

	Business 1	Business 2	Politics 1	Politics 2
Business 1	0.9950	0.3402	0.0221	0.0076
Business 2	0.2333	0.9950	0.0613	0.0328
Politics 1	0.0194	0.0778	0.9950	0.1881
Politics 2	0.0135	0.0493	0.1851	0.9950

The second and third experiments were performed to evaluate the performance of the similarity measure in a clustering task. The second experiment was performed using transcripts from TDT 2 Careful Transcription Text Corpus, LDC catalog number LDC2000T44 [27]. The TDT2 corpus was created to support three TDT2 tasks: find topically homogeneous sections (segmentation), detect the occurrence of new events (detection), and track the reoccurrence of old or new events (tracking). The corpus contains 540 transcriptions of the broadcast news from ABC and CNN from January through June 1998 and of Voice of America (VOA) news broadcasts from March through June 1998.

For our experiment we selected an arbitrary subset of transcripts from the TDT 2 corpus. These were manually clustered. The set of selected documents contained 202 documents with an average length of 72 words per document. The collection of treated documents is available at *http://ieelab-secs.secs.oakland.edu*. Then we applied our algorithm to the same set of transcripts to obtain the clusters of documents automatically. The clusters thus obtained were compared with clusters formed manually to determine the precision and recall values. Table 3 presents the results for one group of topics. Examples of documents appearing in one of the clusters mentioned in Table 3 are given in figure 3. The transcript in the top box is the story most representative the cluster shown. The transcripts in the other boxes are two other stories from the same cluster.

One of the uses of transcript clustering is to identify topics and events in an archived collection of news stories. The main difference between a topic and an event is that an event refers to a group of related incidences that occur in a

Table 3.

Topic	Precision	Recall
Iraq, UN Sanctions	100%	100%
Iraq, M.Albright Talks	100%	100%
US Actions Against Iraq	100%	100%
M.Lewinsky, B.Clinton	100%	85.8%
India, Nuclear Bomb	100%	100%
Stock Market Reports	100%	100%
Weather Reports, Storm	100%	100%

Cluster 32 : Stock Market reports(9 documents)

CNN19980114.1600.1011.utf sim=0.995 <Snapshot>

> In fact, a second wind of sorts in the stock market this afternoon, the final hour of trading, by the closing bell the Dow Jones Industrials finished near their highs of the day up fifty-two and a half points at seventy-seven eighty-four in very active trading. The broader market indices all posted gains as well, and the NASDAQ composite continuing to move higher, it is up six and half points. Shares of Intel, however, fell one and a half at seventy-five and seven-sixteenths after the chip giant said its profit margins will shrink in the near term.

CNN19980108.2130.0960.utf sim=0.197

> With the Asian markets still losing ground, the Dow Jones industrial average took a sharp dive today, falling ninety-nine points to close at seventy-eight oh two.

CNN19980126.1600.1022.utf sim=0.299

> In any case blue chip stocks breaking a three day losing streak. Investors remain cautious and kept the Dow Jones Industrials in moderate rate trading range for most of the day. The Dow did manage to close higher by twelve points, at seventy-seven twelve. The broader markets closed however mostly lower, weakness in the technology sector dragging the NASDAQ composite down fourteen points. And bonds surged as the dollar gained strength, the thirty year treasury up one and four thirty-seconds of a point in price. That has the yield back down to five point eighty-nine percent.

Fig. 3. Subset of documents appeared in Stock Market Reports cluster

narrow spatiotemporal window. In contrast a topic implies a group of events with common theme. With this distinction in mind it would be more appropriate to characterize the rows of Table 3 as indicative of events rather than topics although we did not use any explicit temporal information. For example there are several stories related to topic "Iraq" but we are able to separate them into three distinctive sets of stories. In fact, the results of Table 3 are comparable to those reported by Yang et al [26] using the TDT1 corpus.

The third experiment was designed to see how well the suggested similarity measure and the clustering procedure would work with very poorly transcribed documents. Twenty five audio news clips with original transcripts were selected from the internet. Each clip was then transcribed using four separately trained versions of IBM ViaVoice. These versions were trained by two young male and two young female speakers of different ethnic background. Thus, a total of 125 transcripts, five per story consisting of one original and four noisy versions, were available for experimentation. A summary of the quality of the transcripts thus collected is shown in Table 4.

Table 4.

	Model 1	Model 2	Model 3	Model 4
Average rate	48.96%	48.68%	91.36%	54.76%
Best rate	24%	28%	36%	30%
Worse rate	70%	80%	100%	95%

An original transcript and its best and worst transcribed versions are shown in figure 4. The 125 transcripts were then clustered. This yielded a total of 53 clusters. 25 of these clusters were found to have at least two documents; the remaining 28 clusters were singletons. 22 of the 25 clusters of multiple documents were formed by the different versions of the same transcript. Of the 28 singleton clusters 22 were formed by transcripts corresponding to Model 3 speaker whose average error rate was 91.36%. These results clearly demonstrate that Chi-square similarity measure and the clustering procedure described above are effective even when the transcription is marred by a very high error rate.

We also repeated experiment 3 by using Porter's algorithm [28] for stemming in place of the dictionary look up scheme. This was done to see if a substantial difference in the results would ensue because of a different stemming process. In this case 48 clusters were formed. Once again, 25 of these clusters had two or more documents and 20 of these clusters were formed by the different versions of the same transcript. Of the 22 singleton clusters, 18 were due to Model 3 speaker. These results indicate that the suggested approach works well with the Porter stemming algorithm.

Original document: Politics 14.txt

> To mix metaphors, Orrin Hatch likes to compare it to natural gas, that it's going to find a precipice, some kind of place to come out. John McCain is more optimistic. His view is that this is the gateway to the ability of Congress to work its will on so many other issues where there may be consensuses in the middle that are being blocked by the kind of influence that money can buy.

The best transcript: Pol_14_model_4.txt, Word-Error Rate - 38%

> third to mix metaphors outboard Hatch likes to save the via competitive their natural gas that you you could find a present themselves and I pledge John Kane - think is more optimistic and his feelings that this is the gateway to the ability of Congress to work its will sell many other issues would remain be consensuses in a middle of being what might the kind of influence that money can box

The worse transcript: Pol_14_model_3.txt, Word-Error Rate - 76%

> Porsche of life and Jonathan R. think is more optimistic this isn't . wary to the ability of Congress to work and will Solomon and others choose where the Americans concerns of Susan Mills the ravine wall art a carnival

Fig. 4. The original, best and worst transcribed versions of a document

5 Summary

A method to measure similarity between documents has been presented in this work. The suggested similarity measure is designed to cope with imperfectly transcribed documents. A method for clustering of the documents was also presented and applied to two sets of transcribed documents of varying quality. The results suggest that the suggested similarity measure and the clustering method are capable of achieving high precision and recall rates even in the presence of a high transcription error rate. The method has been also tested for solving TDT tasks on a collection of LDC documents and showed high performance.

We are in the process of further evaluation of the suggested approach and its application to multimedia document indexing and retrieval.

Acknowledgments. The support of Philips Research is gratefully acknowledged.

References

1. U. Gargi, R. Kasturi, and S.H. Strayer, Performance characterization of video-shot-change detection methods. In IEEE Transaction on Circuits and Systems for Video Technology, Vol. 10, No.1, pp. 1-13, February 2000.

2. N. Patel and IK Sethi, Video Shot Detection and Characterization for Video Databases. In Pattern Recognition, Vol. 30, pp. 583-592, April 1997.
3. M.M. Yeung and B.-L. Yeo, Video visualization for compact presentation and fast browsing of pictorial content. In IEEE Transaction on Circuits and Systems for Video Technology, Vol. 7, No. 5, pp. 771-785, October 1997.
4. K.Y. Kupeev and Z. Sivan, An algorithm for efficient segmentation and selection of representative frames in video sequences. In Proceedings of SPIE Conference on Storage and Retrieval for Media Databases, pp. 253-261, San Jose, USA, January 2000.
5. Y.P. Tan, S.R. Kulkarni, and P.J. Ramadge, Rapid estimation of camera motion from compressed video with application to video annotation. In IEEE Transaction on Circuits and Systems for Video Technology, Vol. 10, No. 1, pp. 133-146, February 2000.
6. H.D. Wactler, A.G. Hauptmann, M.G. Christel, R.A. Houghton, and A.M. Olligschlaeger, Complementary video and audio analysis for broadcast news archives. In Communications of the ACM, Vol. 43, No. 2, pp. 42-47, February 2000.
7. T. Sato, T. Kanade, E.K. Hughes, M.A. Smith, and S. Satoh, Video ocr: indexing digital news libraries by recognition of superimposed captions. In Multimedia Systems, Vol. 7, pp. 385-394, 1999.
8. S. Tsekeridou and I. Pitas, Audio-visual content analysis for content-based video indexing. In Proceedings IEEE International Conference on Multimedia Computing and Systems, pp. 667-672, Florence, Italy, June 1999.
9. E. Wold, T. Blum, et al., Content-based classification, search, and retrieval of audio. In IEEE Multimedia, pp. 27-36, Fall 1996.
10. N. V. Patel and I. K. Sethi, Audio characterization for video indexing. In Proceedings of IS&T/SPIE Conf. Storage and Retrieval for Image and Video Databases IV, pp. 373-384, San Jose, CA, February 1996.
11. M. Spina and V. W. Zue, Automatic Transcription of General Audio Data: Preliminary Analyses. In Proceedings of International Conference on Spoken Language Processing, pp. 594-597, Philadelphia, Pa., October 1996.
12. N. V. Patel and I. K. Sethi, Video Classification using Speaker Identification. In Proceedings of IS&T/SPIE Conf. Storage and Retrieval for Image and Video Databases V, pp. 218-225, San Jose, February 1997.
13. Dongge Li, IK Sethi, N Dimitrova and T McGee, Classification of General Audio Data for Content-Based Retrieval. In Pattern Recognition Letters, Vol. 22, pp. 533-544, April 2001.
14. A.G. Hauptmann, M.J. Witbrock, Informedia news on demand: Information acquisition and retrieval, In M.T. Maybury (ed.) Intelligent Multimedia Information Retrieval, AAAI Press/MIT Press, 1997, pp. 213-239.
15. Anni R. Coden, Eric W. Brown, Speech Transcript Analysis for Automatic Search, In IBM Research Report, RC 21838 (98287), September 2000.
16. Proceedings of the sixth Text REtrieval Conference (TREC-6), Gaithersburg, Maryland, November 19-21, 1997.
17. Proceedings of the seventh Text REtrieval Conference (TREC-7), Gaithersburg, Maryland, November 09-11, 1998.
18. Proceedings of the eighth Text REtrieval Conference (TREC-8) held in Gaithersburg, Maryland, November 17-19, 1999.
19. John S. Garofolo, Cedric G.P. Auzanne, Ellen M. Voorhees, The TREC Spoken Document Retrieval Track: A Success Story, In 1999 TREC-8 Spoken Document Retrieval Track Overview and Results, 2000.

20. D. Li, G. Wei, I.K. Sethi, and N. Dimitrova, Fusion of Visual and Audio Features for Person Identification in Real Video, In Proc. Of the SPIE/IS&T Conference on Storage and Retrieval for Media Databases, pp. 180-186, San Jose, California, January 2001.
21. S.E. Robertson, K. Sparck Jones, Simple, Proven Approaches to Text Retrieval, http://www.uky.edu/ gbenoit/637/SparckJones1.html
22. M.Singler, R.Jin, A.Hauptmann, CMU Spoken Document Retrieval in Trec-8: Analysis of the role of Term Frequency TF. In The 8th Text REtrieval Conference, NIST, Gaithersburg, MD, November 1999.
23. D. Abberley, S. Renals, G. Cook, Retrieval of broadcast news documents with the THISL system. In Proc. of the IEEE International Conference on Acoustic, Speech, and Signal Processing, pp. 3781-3784, 1998.
24. S.E. Johnson, P. Jourlin, G.L. Moore, K.S. Jones, P.C. Woodland, The Cambridge University Spoken Document Retrieval System. In Proc. of the IEEE International Conference on Acoustic, Speech, and Signal Processing, pp. 49-52, 1999.
25. R. Willet, Recent trends in hierarchic document clustering: a critical view. In Information Processing and Management., 25(5):577-597, 1988.
26. Y. Yang, J.G. Carbonell, R. Brown, Thomas Pierce, Brian T. Archibald, and Xin Liu, Learning approaches for detecting and tracking news events. In IEEE Intelligent Systems, 14(4):32–43, 1999. http://citeseer.nj.nec.com/yang99learning.html
27. http://www.ldc.upenn.edu/Catalog/TDT.html
28. M.F. Porter, An algorithm for suffix stripping. In Program, 14(3), pp. 130-137, 1980.

Extracting Keyphrases from Spoken Audio Documents

Alain Désilets, Berry de Bruijn, and Joel Martin*

National Research Council of Canada, Bldg M-50, Montreal Road,
Ottawa, Ont, K1A 0R6, Canada
alain.desilets@nrc.ca
berry.debruijn@nrc.ca
joel.martin@nrc.ca

Abstract. Spoken audio documents are becoming more and more common on the World Wide Web, and this is likely to be accelerated by the widespread deployment of broadband technologies. Unfortunately, speech documents are inherently hard to browse because of their transient nature. One approach to this problem is to label segments of a spoken document with keyphrases that summarise them. In this paper, we investigate an approach for automatically extracting keyphrases from spoken audio documents. We use a keyphrase extraction system (Extractor) originally developed for text, and apply it to errorful Speech Recognition transcripts, which may contain multiple hypotheses for each of the utterances. We show that keyphrase extraction is an "easier" task than full text transcription and that keyphrases can be extracted with reasonable precision from transcripts with Word Error Rates (WER) as high as 62%. This robustness to noise can be attributed to the fact that keyphrase words have a lower WER than non-keyphrase words and that they tend to have more redundancy in the audio. From this we conclude that keyphrase extraction is feasible for a wide range of spoken documents, including less-than-broadcast casual speech. We also show that including multiple utterance hypotheses does not improve the precision of the extracted keyphrases.

1   Introduction

The amount of audio and video data available online has been increasing in recent years. Right now, most of this content is of a type commonly known as "multimedia assets" (ex: news broadcasts). Such content is characterised by relatively high production costs and long term value. Therefore, owners of multimedia assets can afford to invest significant resources into manually tagging and indexing this content to make it searchable and browsable online.

---
* We would like to thank Peter Turney for his helpful insights regarding the Extractor system. Thanks also to Bruno Emond who reviewed an early draft of the paper, and to 6 anonymous reviewers whose comments resulted in a much improved paper

Widespread deployment of broadband technologies will likely accelerate the growth of online multimedia content because it will allow more people to use or even produce and distribute such content. Indeed, broadband technologies may cause an explosion of multimedia content, similar to what the World Wide Web did for textual content. However, this next big wave of online multimedia content will probably be of a more "casual" nature such as: home videos or records of videoconferences, meetings and lectures. While there is definitely value in being able to search and access this kind of content online, it probably doesn't warrant manual indexing and it will therefore have to be indexed in a more cost effective and automatic fashion.

Unfortunately, indexing, searching, and browsing of textual context at the scale of the World Wide Web continues to challenge Information Retrieval (IR) researchers, in spite of decades of research. In the case of audio and video content, challenges are even greater because there is no machine palatable way to link the document's representation (or parts of it) to semantically meaningful concepts. In text for example, a machine can easily associate the character string ['d', 'o', 'g'] with the word 'dog' which is itself semantically meaningful. But it cannot do so with a sequence of bits that encodes the acoustic signal of a person saying 'dog' or a bitmap that contains a picture of a dog (at least not with 100% accuracy).

In recent years, thanks to progress in Speech Recognition (SR), significant headway has been made on the front of searching spoken audio documents. The TREC-9 Spoken Document Retrieval track [6,7] , demonstrated that with current SR technology, Word Error Rates (WER) in the order of 27% can be achieved for the Broadcast News (BN) domain. At that level of accuracy, slightly modified versions of the IR techniques devised for text achieve performance comparable to those same methods on error free transcripts. However, Broadcast News is one of the easier domains for this type of technology because the audio is of high quality, and because there are few speech disfluencies such as: filled pauses, false starts, repetition and speech repair. Also, there is an abundance of written news material which can be used for training and query/document expansion. In contrast, the next big wave of online audio will be more casual, which means it will likely be less-than-broadcast quality and exhibit a more conversational speaking style than found in the Broadcast News domain. Also, while a 27% WER seems good enough for the purpose of retrieval, it is not clear how it affects the performance of IR methods for other tasks such as question answering or, in the case of the present paper, keyphrase extraction. A particular issue for keyphrase extraction is that we ultimately want to label portions of audio with written (and potentially errorful) transcriptions of the keyphrases. In contrast, for spoken document retrieval it is usually sufficient to present the user with a link to the original relevant audio document without displaying the errorful transcript that was used to retrieve it.

In this paper, we investigate a technology for extracting keyphrases from spoken documents, which is an adaptation of a system developed for textual content (Extractor system [17,18]). We also evaluate its performance on Broadcast News data, in the face of SR transcripts with different levels of WER.

2   Related Work in Summarisation of Spoken Audio

Speech is inherently more difficult to browse and skim than text because of its transient nature. As Arons [1] puts it: "the ear cannot skim the temporal domain the way the eyes can browse in the spatial domain". This problem has been observed in empirical studies of voicemail users [8,13] . In those papers, the authors conclude that browsing of spoken audio would be greatly facilitated by the use of semantically meaningful signposts for specific sections of the message (ex: greeting, caller identification, and topic). One way to provide such meaningful signposts would be to label each segment in the audio with keyphrases that summarise it.

In the context of spoken audio, summarisation has not been studied as thoroughly as retrieval. Early work [1] focused on acoustic methods to do time compression of the speech without decreasing intelligibility. While they provide an accelerated (but pitch accurate) playback of the original speech, these methods do not provide true summarisation because from a semantic (as opposed to acoustic) perspective, 100% of the original content is still present in the compressed speech.

More recently, advances in SR led to the development of word based approaches that only retain significant parts of the SR transcription of a spoken audio document [2,3,10,11,12,19,20]. Types of summaries that were studied were either single key words [10,11,12,19], short keyphrases (2-3 words) [2], [3] or longer passages of 10 words or more [19,20]. The features used to identify the most relevant segments from the SR transcription were: *acoustic confidence* (i.e. the likelihood that the segment was correctly recognised) [2,3,19,20], significance (i.e. the likelihood that the segment carries important information) [2,3,10,11,12, 19,20] and *prosody* (e.g. pitch, energy, duration, pauses) [2,3,11]. Methods that have been used to select the most relevant segments include *tfidf* [2,3,19], *MMR* [20], *LSI* [12], *lexical chaining* [10], ROC [11] and shallow parsing [2,3]. The audio corpuses used ranged from low quality (*voicemail* [11], videoconference [10], and recording of phone calls [3]) to high quality *Broadcast News* [2,3,12,19,20].

The results of those papers collectively demonstrate that:

a) Significant words tend to have a lower Word Error Rate (WER) than insignificant ones [19,20]
b) Summaries extracted from errorful SR transcripts retain enough important information to be retrievable with an accuracy comparable to retrieval based on a perfect transcription of the whole document [12,19]
c) Those summaries exhibit significant overlaps with human generated summaries [2,3,11,20]
d) Those summaries can improve the performance of users involved in video searching and browsing activities [10]

By "significant words", we mean words that tend to be included in summaries generated automatically using IR methods.

In a sense, points b) and c) are expected corollaries of point a). One may conjecture that speakers have a natural tendency to better articulate parts of the speech which carries important information (limited support for this hypothesis is given by [15]). It may also be that significant words tend to be longer than insignificant words, and that they are correspondingly easier to recognise. Yet another possible explanation is that significant words occur redundantly in the audio and there is a greater chance that some of those occurrences will be recognised correctly. For example, consider a non stop word X which appears 10 times in a short spoken document. Even if the WER for X is fairly high - say 40%, the number of occurrences of the correct transcription of X (6 in this case) might be enough to bring it into the summary. In that case, a user looking only at the summary would see a 0% WER for X instead of the 40% it actually had in the full transcript. In [19] and [20], it is not clear which part those two phenomena (better articulation and higher frequency) played in the lower WER of significant words, because the authors do not specify whether they computed the WER of significant words in the summary only (0% in our example) or in the whole transcript (40% in our example). However, as we will discuss later, our own experiments show that significant words have lower WER even when the effect of their higher frequency is eliminated (see section 5).

In this paper, we investigate a technology for extracting keyphrases from spoken audio documents. Here by keyphrase, we mean a short sequence of consecutive words (typically 1 to 3) that capture an important theme of the speech. Previous work on word-based speech summarisation mostly studied either single keywords or longer summaries such as utterances or N-grams (N > 10). The advantage of keyphrases over keywords is that they provide more precise descriptors of the themes in a document. For example, the phrase *"genetic algorithm"* is more precise than either *"genetic"* or *"algorithm"*, or even the keyword set { *"genetic"*, *"algorithm"* } (the later could equally refer to genetic algorithms or to algorithms for mining genomic data). Yet, because keyphrases are still fairly concise, they are better suited than longer summaries for tasks such as signposting of audio segments.

Another aim of our work is to investigate the quality of keyphrases that can be extracted from SR transcripts with very high WER (in the order of 60-65%). To date, most of the literature on speech summarisation [2,10,11,12,19] looked at SR transcripts with WERs in the 20-40% range (except for [3] and [20] which looked at the 25-50% WER range). Knowing how far we can stretch the envelope while maintaining summary quality is important because it allows us to handle more diverse types of audio recordings.

In the remaining sections, we describe our approach to extracting keyphrases from spoken audio, based on the Extractor system developed for text by Turney [17,18]. We also describe experiments that evaluate the performance of the system on broadcast and "simulated" less-than-broadcast audio.

3   Extracting Keyphrases from Speech with Extractor

Our approach to extracting keyphrases from spoken audio is based on the Extractor system developed for text by Turney. Extractor uses a supervised learning approach to maximise overlap between machine extracted and human extracted keyphrases.

The Extractor algorithm works as follows. For each phrase (i.e. a sequence of 1 to 3 consecutive words) in a document, Extractor computes a score representing the system's confidence that it is a keyphrase. The score is computed based on a series of features of the phrase such as: *frequency* of occurrence, position of the *first occurrence* in the text and *length* of the phrase. A series of 12 parameters determines how those features are combined to obtain the final confidence score. These parameters are tuned automatically by a genetic algorithm whose goal is to maximise the overlap between machine and human extracted keyphrases. Evaluation of the various possible tunings by the genetic algorithm is done using a training corpus for which humans have already extracted keyphrases.

Extractor has been tested on a wide range of corpuses (scientific literature, email messages and web pages). Average precision (defined here as the percent of machine keyphrases that were also extracted by humans) on those corpuses ranged between 20-30%. This may appear low, but it is comparable to the level of agreement found between different humans indexing the same documents [5]. Another study [18] showed that 80% of the keyphrases generated by Extractor are deemed acceptable by human readers. So far, Extractor has been licensed to 15 companies that have used it for a variety of applications including: summarisation of web sites to assist webmasters, summarising email messages for display on short messaging devices and plugins for summarising documents inside office productivity suites.

Table 1. Characteristics of evaluation data

	Source Type	Num. Stories
ABC	TV	42
PRI	Radio	58
All sources	mixed	100

Our first attempt at adapting Extractor to spoken audio documents uses the most straightforward approach one can think of. We simply present Extractor with a transcription containing the top-N SR hypotheses for each of the utterances in the audio. The rationale for using N > 1 hypotheses is that even if a keyphrase is not correctly recognised in the "best" hypothesis, it might be correctly recognised in one of the remaining N - 1 hypotheses. The use of multiple hypotheses has been investigated in various papers on Spoken Document Retrieval (for example, [14,16]), but so far, only one paper looked at it for summarisation [3]. Another indirect effect of this approach is to boost the score of phrases that have a high acoustic confidence. This is because words with high acoustic confidence will tend to appear in more than one of the top-N hypotheses for the same utterance, and therefore their frequency of occurrence in the transcription will be higher (and frequency is an important feature in Extractor's scoring scheme).

As we will now demonstrate, this simple approach turns out to perform very well even in conditions where WER is high.

4   The Experiments

We conducted experiments to evaluate the performance of Extractor in the Broadcast News domain, using a subset of the ABC and PRI stories of the TDT2 English Audio data. We only used stories that had human generated careful transcripts (i.e. exact transcripts as opposed to closed-caption transcripts which sometimes paraphrase the speech). Table 1 lists the characteristics of this data.

We ran Extractor on five kinds of transcripts :

- error-free careful transcripts (CR)
- paraphrased closed-caption transcripts (CC)
- moderate WER SR transcripts with only the best hypothesis for each utterance (MSR)
- a series of high WER SR transcript with the top N hypotheses for each utterance (HSR-N, N=1,..., 10)

Table 2. Characteristics of the various transcripts

	Generated by	Num. Hyp.	WER (%)		
			ABC	PRI	all
CR	Humans	1	0.0	0.0	0.0
CC	Humans (closed-caption)	1	14.1	8.6	11
MSR	NIST/BBN	1	21.5	32.4	27.6
HSR-1	Dragon Naturally Speaking	1	58.8	65.0	62.3
HSR-N (N>1)	Dragon Naturally Speaking	N	N/A	N/A	N/A

The characteristics of those transcripts are summarised in Table 2. Figure 1 shows examples of CR, MSR, HSR-1 and HSR-5 for a same news story.

CR corresponds to the error-free careful transcripts produced manually for a small random sample of the TDT2 corpus. We used those transcripts as a reference to evaluate the WER of SR transcripts, and to evaluate the precision of keyphrases extracted from those transcripts.

CC corresponds to the closed-caption transcripts for the stories. They are not 100% error free since they often paraphrase content to make the transcript more concise. However, the "errors" are usually meaning preserving. We used the CC transcript to get an idea of the rate of false negatives when using CR extracted keyphrases as a base for assessing the relevance of keyphrases extracted from other transcripts. A false negative in this context is a case where a keyphrase extracted from a SR transcript turns out to be a good keyphrase even though it was not extracted from the corresponding CR transcript. Because CC and CR transcripts have essentially the same semantic content (but slightly different textual content), there is no reason to think that keyphrases extracted from CC are any less relevant than keyphrases extracted from CR. Therefore the difference between the two sets of keyphrases gives us an estimate of the rate of false negatives (as defined above).

MSR corresponds to the B1 (baseline) transcripts generated for the TREC-8 SDR Track [7], using the NIST/BBN time-adaptive speech recognizer. These transcripts had a moderate WER (27.6%) which is representative of what can be obtained with a state of the art SR system tuned for the Broadcast News domain.

HSR-N transcripts were obtained using Dragon's NaturallySpeaking speaker dependent recogniser. The WER of HSR-1 (62.3%) was much higher than MSR because the voice model used was not trained for speaker independent broadcast quality audio. The WER for HSR-N, N > 1 could not be computed since such a transcript is not comparable to a reference transcript with only one hypothesis per utterance. We used the HSR-N transcripts to (i) simulate the type of high WER one might expect with more casual less-than-broadcast quality audio, and (ii) investigate how taking multiple hypotheses into account might address that higher WER.

With Extractor, we generated 5 keyphrases for each SR transcript and 10 for the CR transcripts. We used two types of relevance judgments which we call *surrogate* and *human relevance*. In *surrogate relevance*, keyphrases extracted from a SR transcript were deemed relevant if they appeared in the list of 10 keyphrases extracted from the corresponding CR transcript. Note that we compared stemmed phrases (using the Lovins stemming algorithm) so that a phrase like "data mining" would match "data mine". Surrogate relevance implicitly assumes that Extractor is a perfect surrogate for human judgment, which is not completely realistic. Based on previous studies of Extractor [18] we would expect this surrogate evaluator to have a 20% false positive error rate. We do not have estimates for the false negative error rate. However, we would expect it to be fairly high, especially for longer stories. This is because long stories may contain many relevant keyphrases while the surrogate judge never considers more than 10 phrases to be relevant.

Human relevance was based on actual relevance judgments by one of the experimenters. These human judgments may be more favorable than surrogate

CR

And Belfast's annual marathon was rerouted today after a mortar attack against a police station nearby. Police said two devices had exploded, but caused no damage or injuries. In the _B_B_C news room, I'm Kimberly Dozier for The World.

MSR

and belfast annual marathon was read about it today after a mortar attack against a police station nearby police said two devices had exploded but caused no damage or injuries and the b. b. c. newsroom I'm kimberly goes your for the world

HSR-1

to annual marathon was and we landed today after a border attack against the police station nearby police into devices had exploited across the damage or injuries and BBC Israel and Kimberly Dozier of the world !

HSR-5

to annual marathon was and we landed today after a border attack against the police station nearby police into devices had exploited across the damage or injuries and BBC Israel and Kimberly Dozier of the world .

to annual marathon was and we landed today after a border attack against the police station nearby police into devices had exploited across their damage or injuries and BBC Israel and Kimberly Dozier of the world .

to annual marathon was and we landed today after a border attack against the police station nearby police into devices had exploited across the damage or injury is the BBC Israel and Kimberly Dozier of the world .

to annual marathon was and we landed today after a border attack against the police station nearby police into devices had exploited across their damage or injury is the BBC Israel and Kimberly Dozier of the world .

to annual marathon was and we landed today after a border attack against the police station nearby police into devices headaches bloodied but Costner damage or injuries and BBC Israel and Kimberly Dozier of the world.

Fig. 1. Sample transcripts for a PRI story

relevance for both legitimate and illegitimate reasons. One legitimate reason is that the human judge might find a keyphrase "President Bill Clinton" to be relevant while the surrogate judgment was negative because Extractor found "Bill Clinton" instead. Also, even for long stories our surrogate evaluator only considered 10 keyphrase as being relevant, whereas the human evaluator had no such limit. The illegitimate reason is of course that the experimenter may have had an unconscious favorable bias regarding the quality of the extracted keyphrases.

We used both types of relevance to evaluate the average precision of the keyphrases. Recall was not evaluated, because in the context of summarisation there is no clear definition of what constitutes a complete recall set. The complete set of relevant keyphrases for a document really depends on the level of summarisation that is desired and one cannot say that a set of 5 keyphrases is less complete than a superset of, say, 20 keyphrases.

5   Discussion

First we look at the WER of words in the extracted keyphrases versus the WER of the whole transcripts. Table 3 lists the WERs of both keyphrase words and whole transcripts for the various SR transcripts. Like previous studies [19,20],

Table 3. WER of keyphrases and transcripts

	% WER (keyphrases/transcripts)		
	ABC	**PRI**	**all**
MSR	16.9 / 21.5	26.8 / 32.4	22.6 / 27.6
HSR-1	55.1 / 58.8	58.5 / 65.0	57.0 / 62.3

we found the WER of keyphrase words to be lower than the WER of the corresponding transcripts. However, we found the differences to be more marginal (3.7-6.5%) than what was found in [19] (which was in the order of 12%). In [20] the authors only reported correlation between the tfidf and acoustic scores of words and said nothing about the magnitude of the differences, so we cannot compare our findings to theirs. Note also that we computed the WER of every occurrence of the keyphrase words, so that a word which had 6 correct occurrences and 4 incorrect ones would have a WER of 40%, even if the version presented in the list of extracted keyphrases was the correct transcription. This means that the difference between WER of keyphrase and non-keyphrases cannot be attributed to the fact that keyphrases occur more often in the text (which as we pointed out in Section 2, might not have been the case in [19] and [20].

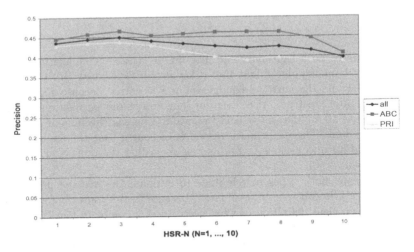

Fig. 2. Surrogate precision of keyphrases as a function of number of hypotheses in transcript

Next, we look at the effect of including N > 1 utterance hypotheses in the transcripts. Figure 2 plots the surrogate precision of keyphrases as a function of the number of hypotheses in the HSR transcripts, for each of the audio sources. All 3 curves exhibit a slight downward trend as N increases.

However, this apparent trend was not found to be significant. Results of a linear regression show that the slope of all three curves is not statistically different from 0, which indicates neither improvement nor degradation of performance as N was increased. We also did a series of paired t-tests ($p > .95$) comparing N=1 to each of the N > 1 for each of the curves, and found that only N=7 and N=10 for the PRI curve were statistically worse than N=1. From this, we conclude that taking into account multiple hypotheses with the simple approach we studied does not help with keyphrase extraction. This is consistent with results reported in [3]. Consequently, in the rest of the discussion we will focus on results for HSR-1.

Looking at the sample HSR-1 and HSR-5 transcripts in Fig.1, we can see why additional SR hypotheses do not improve performance. In this sample, the alternate hypotheses are very similar to the first one, and they differ only in unimportant words. Figure 3 shows that this trend is also present in the whole corpus. It plots the average normalised number of occurrences of good keyphrases in the various HSR-N transcripts. By good keyphrases, we mean those keyphrases which were automatically extracted from the perfect CR. By normalised number of occurrences, we mean the number of occurrence divided by N. Since the length of the transcripts grows linearly with N, this measure is proportional to the relative frequency (i.e. number of occurrences divided by length of transcript). The fact that all three curves are flat means that on average, good keyphrases do not occur more nor less frequently in the N > 1 hypotheses than in the N=1 hypothesis.

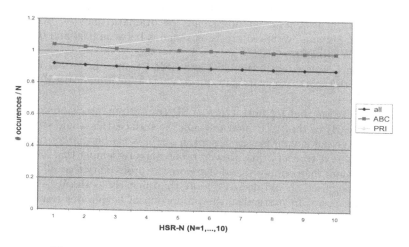

Fig. 3. Frequency of good keyphrases in HSR-N (N=1,...10)

We now look at how precision of the extracted keyphrases degrades as the level of WER increases. Table 4 lists the observed surrogate and human precision of keyphrases for the various types of transcripts.

The MSR row in Table 4 shows that the performance of Extractor is only mildly affected by the level of WER that can be obtained on Broadcast News with a state of the art SR system trained for that domain. This is true for both surrogate and human precision. Note also that both overall precision figures for HSN (0.77 and 0.74) are just slightly less than the 80% figure found previously for keyphrases extracted by Extractor from errorless text [18]. Another indication that Extractor is doing well on MSR is that surrogate precision on those transcripts is comparable to the surrogate precision on the CC transcripts. This means that the percentage of MSR keyphrases that were rejected by the surrogate relevance judgments is within the rate of false negatives of those surrogate judgments (which, as we pointed out in Section 4, can be estimated by the differences between CC and CR extracted keyphrases).

Table 4. Precision of keyphrases from various transcripts (surrogate / human)

	ABC	PRI	all
CC	0.83 / NA	0.80 / NA	0.81 / NA
MSR	0.86 / 0.85	0.72 / 0.67	0.77 / 0.74
HSR-1	0.45 / 0.60	0.44 / 0.50	0.44 / 0.54

Looking at the performance of Extractor on transcripts with high WER (HSR-1 row), we see a significant drop in both observed precision measures. However, the drop in human precision is less dramatic than the drop in surrogate precision. Human evaluated precision remains between 0.50 and 0.60 in spite of average WERs of up to 62.3%.

In Fig.4, we aggregate the MSR and HSR-1 transcripts at 5% WER intervals and plot the aggregated surrogate precision as a function of WER for both MSR and HSR-1.

We observe that for both types of SR transcripts, precision decreases somewhat linearly as the WER increases. On the surface, this would seem to indicate that extracting keyphrases from spoken audio is neither harder nor easier than doing full-text transcription. However, one must remember that keyphrases may contain more than one word and therefore the probability that all words are correctly recognised should decrease more than linearly as the WER of individual words increases. In particular, the proportion of keyphrases that are correctly recognised should be:

$$\left(\frac{1}{n}\right) \sum_k n_k \, (1 - WER)^k \qquad (1)$$

where:

   $k=1,...,3$: number of words in a keyphrase
   n_k: number of keyphrases with k words
   n: total number of keyphrases

The "Correctly Recognised" curve in Fig.4 plots that curve for the values of n_k observed in our data. Since an extracted keyphrase cannot be deemed relevant unless all words in it match a correct keyphrase, we would expect their precision to also decrease more than linearly with WER. In fact this tendency should be worsened by the fact that a relevant extracted keyphrase must be both 100% correctly recognised and be a significant phrase in the audio.

So the linear relationship we observe between keyphrase precision and WER of the full text transcripts is somewhat surprising. The surprisingly high precision can be explained in part by the lower WER of keyphrases which we have observed in the data. However, the higher frequency of keyphrase words may also play a subtle role here.

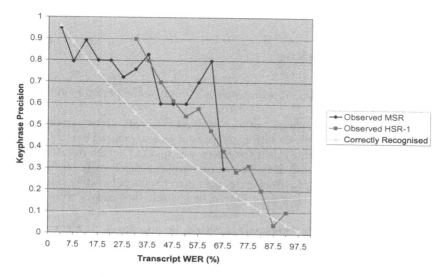

Fig. 4. Surrogate precision of keyphrases as a function of transcript WER

For example, suppose you have a phrase which occurs a great number of times in the audio, and suppose that the correct hypothesis for that phrase has the highest probability. Then the frequency of the various hypotheses in the transcript would closely approximate their probability distribution. The hypothesis with highest frequency in the transcript would then almost always be the correct hypothesis. If you were to select that for inclusion in the list of keyphrases, you would then almost always end up with a correctly recognised extracted keyphrase. In contrast, if there were only a few occurrences of the phrase in the audio, the frequency of the various hypotheses might be further from their probability distribution, and it would be more likely that the hypothesis which occurs most frequently in the transcript is not the correct one.

Note that it is hard to say which of the two phenomena (lower WER or higher frequency) plays the greater role in increasing the precision of extracted keyphrase. This is because Extractor produces keyphrases through a complex, non linear transformation of the features of phrases. But the fact remains that keyphrase extraction turns out to be easier than full text transcription, thanks to some combination of those two factors.

Overall, our experiments show that Extractor is able to produce relevant keyphrases even for transcripts with large WER rates. The question is: "does it perform well enough to be practical"? For the Broadcast News domains, the fact that we achieve precision comparable to what Extractor achieves on errorless text, combined with the fact that Extractor has been used by various licensees to produce successful text summarisation applications, tells us that the answer is probably yes. For more casual less-than-broadcast speech, more work is required to assess whether the level of precision we are getting (45-60%) is good enough for practical applications.

6   Future Work

There are various ways in which we could improve the performance of Extractor on spoken audio.

For example, our simple approach only used the SR acoustic confidence scores indirectly. Because words with high acoustic scores occurred in many hypotheses for any given utterance, their frequency was boosted, which resulted in a corresponding boost in their Extractor score (which relies heavily on frequency). It would be interesting to investigate more direct ways of boosting words based on their acoustic confidence, for example, by treating the acoustic score as a pseudo frequency.

Another possible improvement would be to exploit prosodic information which tends to be correlated with the significance of words in speech [15].

On the front of evaluation, we need to conduct more realistic experiments to assess the performance of Extractor on speech data. For example, the high WER transcripts we used were not obtained from actual less-than-broadcast casual speech. It would be interesting to see how the algorithm performs on transcripts produced from true less-than-broadcast casual speech using a speaker independent system tuned for that domain. We plan to investigate this for audio recording of K-12 lessons, in the context of the LearnCanada project [4].

The relevance judgments used in our experiments were either potentially unrealistic (in the case of the machine generated surrogate judgments) or potentially biased (in the case of the human judgments made by one of the experimenters). We need to conduct additional experiments to evaluate the relevance of extracted keyphrases as perceived by independent human evaluators.

Finally, it would be interesting to investigate the use of automatically extracted keyphrases to help video retrieval and browsing in actual applications. This is particularly necessary for applications to high WER speech where it is not so clear that the level of precision we obtain is good enough to be practical. We plan to investigate this for applications of video annotation and sharing in a K-12 setting [4].

7   Conclusion

In this paper, we studied a technology for the automatic extraction of keyphrases from spoken audio documents. The overall conclusion is that keyphrase extraction is very robust to misrecognition errors and that keyphrases could be extracted with reasonable precision for a wide range of audio quality. In particular, we showed that keyphrases could be extracted with 54% precision from transcripts with as high as 62% Word Error Rates. This robustness can be attributed to the fact that keyphrase words tend to have a lower WER than non keyphrase words, and that they tend to occur redundantly in the audio.

Our experiments also demonstrate that including multiple utterance hypotheses in the transcripts does not improve the precision of the extracted keyphrases. This is attributable to the fact that keyphrases tend to already appear in the first hypothesis, and that their relative frequency tends to remain constant even if additional hypotheses are taken into account.

References

1. Arons, B. Speech Skimmer: Interactively Skimming Recorder Speech. Proc. UIST '93: ACM Symposium on User Interface Software and Technology. ACM Press. Nov 3-5 '93. Atlanta. pp. 187-196.
2. Coden, A., Brown, R. Speech Transcript Analysis for Automatic Search. Proceedings of the 34th Annual Hawaii International Conference on System Sciences. Outrigger Wailea Resort , January 3-6, 2001.
3. Cooper, J. W., Viswanathan, M., Byron, D., Chan, M. Building Searchable Collections of Enterprise Speech Data. First ACM/IEEE-CS joint conference on Digital libraries. June 24 - 28, 2001, Roanoke, VA USA. Pp 226-234.
4. Emond, B. Brooks, M., Smith, A. A Broadband Web-based application for Video Sharing and Annotation, ACM Multimedia, Submitted, 2001.
5. G. W. Furnas, Thomas K. Landauer, L. M. Gomez, and S. T. Dumais. The vocabulary problem in human-system communication. Communications of the ACM, 30(11):964–971, November 1987.
6. Garofolo, J., Lard, J., Voorhes, E. 2000 TREC-9 Spoken Document Retrieval Track. http://www.nist.gov/speech/sdr2000/
7. Garofolo, J., Auzanne, C. G. P., Voorhees, E. The TREC Spoken Document Retrieval Track: A Success Story. RIAO 2000, Content-Based Multimedia Information Access, pp. 1-20, 2000
8. Hirschberg, J., Whittaker, S., Hindle, D., Pereira, F., Singhal, A. Finding Information in Audio: a New Paradigm for Audio Browsing and Retrieval. In Proceeding of the ESCA ETRW Workshop.
9. Hirst G., St-Onge D. Lexical Chains as representation of context for the detection and correction malapropisms. In C. Fellbaum, editor, WordNet: An electronic lexical database and some of its applications. Cambrige, MA: The MIT Press. 1997.
10. Kazman, R., Al-Halimi, R., Hunt, W., and Mantei, M., Four Paradigms for Indexing Video Conferences. IEEE Multimedia, Spring 1996, pp. 63-73.
11. Koumpis, K., Renals, S., Niranjan, M. Extractive Summarization of Voicemail using Lexical and Prosodic Feature Subset Selection. Eurospeech 2001, Aalborg, Denmark, Sept. 2001.

12. Kurimo, M. Fast latent semantic indexing of spoken documents by using self-organizing maps. In Proc. ICASSP, 2000.
13. Nakatani, C., Whittaker,S., Hirshberg, J. Now you hear it, now you don't: Empirical Studies of Audio Browsing Behavior. In Proceedings of the Fifth International Conference on Spoken Language Processing, Sydney, 1998. ICSLP98.
14. M. Siegler, A. Berger, A., M. Witbrock. Experiments in Spoken Document Retrieval at CMU. Proc. TREC-7, November 1998, page 319.
15. Silipo, R., Crestani, F. Acoustic Stress and Topic Detection in American English Spoken Sentences. Technical Report TR-00-005. International Computer Science Institute, Berkeley, Ca. March 2000.
16. Srinivasan, S., Petkovic, D. Phonetic Confusion Matrix Based Spoken Document Retrieval. Proceedings of the 23rd annual international ACM SIGIR conference on Research and development in information retrieval. July 24 - 28, 2000, Athens Greece. pp 81-87.
17. Turney, P. D. Learning to Extract Keyphrases from Text. Technical Report ERB-1057, National Research Council, Institute for Information Technology, 1999.
18. Turney, P. Learning Algorithms for Keyphrase Extraction. Information-Retrieval. vol.2, no.4; 2000; p.303-6
19. R. Valenza, T. Robinson, M. Hickey, and R. Tucker. Summarisation of spoken audio through information extraction. In Proceedings of the ESCA workshop: Accessing information in spoken audio, pages 111-116. Cambridge, UK, April. 1999.
20. K. Zechner and A. Waibel. Minimizing word error rate in textual summaries of spoken language. In Proceedings of NAACL-ANLP-2000, Seattle, WA, May 2000.

Segmenting Conversations by Topic, Initiative, and Style

Klaus Ries*

Interactive Systems Labs
Carnegie Mellon University, Pittsburgh, PA, 15213, USA
Universität Karlsruhe, Fakultät für Informatik, 76128 Karlsruhe,Germany
ries@cs.cmu.edu

Abstract. Topical segmentation is a basic tool for information access to audio records of meetings and other types of speech documents which may be fairly long and contain multiple topics. Standard segmentation algorithms are typically based on keywords, pitch contours or pauses. This work demonstrates that speaker initiative and style may be used as segmentation criteria as well. A probabilistic segmentation procedure is presented which allows the integration and modeling of these features in a clean framework with good results.

Keyword based segmentation methods degrade significantly on our meeting database when speech recognizer transcripts are used instead of manual transcripts. Speaker initiative is an interesting feature since it delivers good segmentations and should be easy to obtain from the audio. Speech style variation at the beginning, middle and end of topics may also be exploited for topical segmentation and would not require the detection of rare keywords.

1 Introduction

Segmenting a dialogue into meaningful units is a problem that has received considerable attention in the past and can be seen as a preprocessing stage to information retrieval [20], summarization [39], anaphora resolution and text/dialogue understanding. This paper uses keyword repetition, speaker initiative and speaking style to achieve topical segmentation of spontaneous dialogues. The intended applications are navigation support for meetings and other everyday rejoinders and preprocessing for applications such as information retrieval. This paper is also an attempt to support the authors general claim that discourse style is an important feature for information access in spoken language as also discussed in other publications [30,31]. A clean probabilistic framework is presented which

---

* I would like to thank my advisor Alex Waibel for supporting and encouraging this work and my collegues for various discoursive and practical contributions, especially Hua Yu and Klaus Zechner. The reviewers provided valuable comments for the final paper presentation. I would also like to thank our sponsors at DARPA. Any opinions, findings and conclusions expressed in this material are those of the authors and do not necessarily reflect the views of DARPA, or any other party.

A.R. Coden, E.W. Brown, and S. Srinivasan (Eds.): IR Techniques ..., LNCS 2273, pp. 51–66, 2002.

allows to formulate keyword repetition and speaker initiative as "coherence features" whereas style is modeled as a "region feature". "Coherence features" are features that have to be coherent within one topical segment – examples are the keyword distribution or speaker initiative. Speaker initiative is encoded by speaker identity for each turn and possibly the information whether the turn is long or short. (see Sec. 6 for a discussion and experiments on the encoding of speaker initiative).

"Region features" on the other hand are designed to model properties of different regions of topical segments such as the boundary and the beginning, middle and end of a topic. Region features are used to model the change in the part of speech distribution which is a stylistic feature. Region features could also be used to encode features such as prosody and pause lengths.

The databases used in the experiments contains everyday rejoinders, meetings and (personal) telephone conversations [1]. The effective access to audio records of this nature could provide more accurate minutes, improve minutes by adding "audio citations" and increase the confidence in the minute construction process [21]. If meeting minutes are not prepared an automatically generated index may improve the access to the document. Meetings and other everyday rejoinders are fairly different from broadcast news data which has been the focus of information access to speech documents in the recent TREC-SDR (information retrieval) [5] and TDT (topic detection and tracking) initiatives. The following key properties are affecting the dialogue segmentation problem:

Speech recognition performance. Typical best practice word error rates for Large Vocabulary Speech Recognition (LVCSR) systems on broadcast news are around 20% [1] for fast decoders in 1998 whereas they are around 40% for slow systems on meeting data in 2001. The most likely explanation would be a significant difference in speaking style of everyday rejoinders from broadcasts.

Domain knowledge. While broadcast news seems to cover a large domain the topics seem to repeat themselves and a lot of information related to the speech document is available in electronic form. The topic repetition property allowed [37] to use only 100 topic models for segmentation while such preconstructed topic models can't be assumed for everyday rejoinders such as meetings. Keywords of everyday rejoinders may be highly ideosynchratic such that they may not be in the vocabulary of an LVCSR system. Even if some keywords are available it is unlikely that one can use online resources for document expansion [33] and vocabulary adaptation [6] which employ cooccurrence information of keywords to enhance information retrieval and speech recognition performance.

Manual cuts and genre constraints. Broadcasts and especially news shows are very specific genres which are designed for mass consumption: News shows for example are cut in short but very distinct stories which are introduced or ended with very specific phrases. If video is present a "cut" is

---

[1] Additionally the publicly available database of a recent publication on topic segmentation [4] is used for comparison.

likely inserted which may be detected easily, narrowing down the number of possible topic boundaries. Everyday conversations on the other hand don't exhibit such clear topical boundaries and topic-shifts may occur gradually.

We have participated in the DoD sponsored Clarity project which dealt with dialogue processing on speech corpora. Given the information above it was unlikely that keywords detected by a speech recognizer would provide good features for topic segmentation. Thus, other features such as speaking style have been investigated. To field products on mobile devices [36] it would be an advantage to eliminate the need for speech recognition altogether since it is expensive.

The paper presents related work (Sec. 2), the definition of topic (Sec. 3), the evaluation metrics (Sec. 4) and the algorithmic framework (Sec. 5). Experimental results are presented in Sec. 6 and conclusions are offered in Sec. 7.

2   Related Work

2.1   Segmentation Criteria

Topic segmentation has been studied by other authors previously and a variety of segmentation criteria have been suggested: [8,9,37] suggest that segments are assumed to contain semantically distinct elements, usually presented by lexical cohesion which is adapted in this work; [24,2] suggest that local features indicate topic shifts; [19] proposes an approach based on rhetorical structure to derive a hierarchical representation of the dialogue; [10,32] show how to use automatically detected prosodic features for segmentation; [35] uses initiative as a manual segmentation criterion and finally multimodal features such as gesture, movement and gaze are used by [27]. Discourse theories such as [7,18] would also be attractive candidates for segmentation of human dialogue and indeed [19] has shown success in parsing rhetorical structure in text domains using keywords and phrases.

The author therefore decided to use the widely studied keyword repetition feature [8,9,37] and speaker initiative as "coherence features". Speaker initiative has so far only been used as a manual segmentation criterion [35]. Speaking style as encoded in the part-of-speech distribution is explored as a "region feature". The suggested algorithm allows the direct integration of "coherence features" as well as "region features". So far algorithm designers have separated the two sets of features or integrated them in a less direct manner.

2.2   Keyword Repetition Algorithms

The part of the algorithm which handles coherence features is related to the approach of [37,28]. [37] assumes that each segment of a conversation is generated by one of a couple of hundred pretrained topics – the algorithm is therefore domain dependent. The algorithm presented here does not make that assumption and is therefore domain independent. The domain independence is achieved by training a model for each segment on the fly instead of relying on pretrained models. An advantage of [37] is that information about semantically related terms is included implicitly. This may be achieved using other techniques such as [25]; however [37,25] techniques rely on the availability of adequate training material which may not be available for everyday discourse or meetings. A fair comparison to [37] is not possible since there is really no topic repetition across dialogues in our databases which would disfavor their approach while the TDT database would require to add synonym handling to this algorithm.

[28] presents the domain independent probabilistic *word frequency algorithm* for topical segmentation. It estimates the probability of a boundary for every location in the text and uses a thresholding technique to derive the actual boundaries. The drawback is that the estimation of the boundaries assumes fixed sized windows around the boundary and the boundary placement is not optimized globally unlike the Viterbi search employed by [37] and the proposed algorithm.

[9] is probably the most widely cited domain independent algorithm for topical segmentation and relies on cosine similarity measures combined with heuristic optimization criteria and optimization procedures. Similar algorithms, applying similar measures with different optimization criteria, are [28,4]. [9,4] were chosen to establish a comparison to existing domain independent algorithms: [9] is known widely and [4] is the most recent publication in this area which compares to [11,28,9].

2.3   Boundary Classification Algorithms

Many algorithmic approaches have used boundary classification: A classifier is trained which has the output "Boundary: Yes/No". Using "region features" the classifier can be extended to produce other outputs for larger regions such as "Begin of topic", "End of topic" and so forth. The UMass approach in [1] seems to model word type information in different regions of topical segments using an HMM model. The model presented here can be trained using a discriminative classifier but imposes a fixed structure of the topical segment.

Since news shows are a highly organized genre following specific scripts very specific topic shift indicators (such as LIVE, C. N. N.) can work very well which was used by [2,10]. Other features studied as topic indicators are keyphrases, pauses and prosodic features such as a preceding low boundary tone or a pitch range reset [10,32,24]. While these may be modeled easily using region features the author hasn't been able to establish good results on the dialogues although the prosody module has been tested successfully on an emotion detection task.

Boundary classification algorithms may also integrate information about the change in the keyword distribution using features similar to most keyword repetition algorithms [2,10]. The critique of this technique is however that it is relying on local, window based changes of the keyword distribution and that the algorithms are not applying a global optimization over all possible sequences [2]. On

---

[2] One may argue that exponential segmentation models [2] may weigh the contribution of the keyword repetition feature with the other models in a principled way. On the other hand the parameterization of the exponential models used may also be

the other hand the algorithm presented in this paper as well as [4,37] integrate keyword information over the complete topical segment.

3   Definition of Topic

A theoretically pleasing definition of topic that could be applied reliably in practice doesn't exist currently. A simple solution is to compose artificial data randomly picking initial segments from different documents which constitute the topics to obtain a database of different topics. This method is used by [4] in his C99-database which is also used in Tab. 1. The problem with that approach is that the modeling of topic length may be artificial and the shifts between topics may not be natural.

However this work is concerned with the segmentation of naturally occurring dialogues in meetings and everyday rejoinders where topic shifts are not that abrupt and uninitiated. [24] discuss the topic definition problem in great detail and the most common way to establish the quality of a definition is a reasonable agreement between human coders (also called "intercoder agreement"). [9] argues that "naive" (largely untrained, linguistically inexperienced) coders generate sufficient agreements compared to trained coders when asked to place segment boundaries between topical segments. The use of naive coders may also be appropriate for work in information retrieval since it may reflect results that could be anticipated from users of an actual retrieval system. The topic definition applied in this work instructs the coders to place a boundary where the topic changes or the speakers engage in a different activity such as discussing, storytelling etc. The activities were annotated at the same time as the topic segmentation was produced [30,31]. The primary annotation for all databases was done by semi-naive subjects. Some had considerable experience annotating the databases with dialogue features however no special linguistic training or criteria were provided for the topic segmentation task beyond the definition of activities.

The meeting database was also segmented by the author. The intercoder agreement was measured by (a) treating the second human similar to a machine using the standard evaluation metric (Sec. 4, Table 2), (b) measuring κ for the boundary/non-boundary distinction for each utterance ($\kappa = 0.36$) and (c) measuring κ for the distinction of links [3] as *within topic / across topic* ($\kappa = 0.35$). The κ-statistics [3] therefore indicates that the intercoder agreement is relatively low overall which is not surprising given the difficulty of the task. The result seems to be in the same range as other similar annotations [24].

---

interpreted as a different weighting scheme between "coherence features" and "region features". A pilot experiment using a couple of settings did not indicate any change of the segmentation accuracy.

[3] Refer to Sec. 4 for the description of links.

4   Evaluation Methods

A standard evaluation metric for text segmentation has been suggested by [2,1]. The metric is fairly intuitive and [2] argues that it is fairly robust against simple cheating attempts. The intuition behind the metric is that a segmentation is good if two words that belong to the same topic in the reference belong to the same topic in the hypothesis.

More specifically if two words have distance k they form a *link*. A link is called *within topic* if the two words belong to the same topic, otherwise it is across topic. If the corresponding links in the hypothesis and reference are both *within topic* or both *across topic* the hypothesis is correct, otherwise it is an error. The reported metric is the average link error rate in percent. For each database, k is half the average topic length of the database.

All speech databases have been manually segmented based on the manual transcripts. The results for automatic transcripts of the meeting database have been obtained by transferring the manual topic segmentation to the results generated by the speech recognizer. The speech recognition system segments the input by pause length. Based on time stamps the next best utterance beginning is chosen as the segment boundary.

[4] calculates the link error rate differently and his technique is used when reporting results on the C99-database. The first step in his procedure is to calculate the average link error rate for every text in the database. The link length k for every text is determined as half the average topic length of the respective text. The average link error rate of a database is the average of the average link error rate of all texts in the database.

As a baseline an "equal distance segmentation" is being used, similar to B_e in [4]. The dialogue is segmented into utterances with equal sized topics of length d where d is the average length of a topic in a training set. The parameter d is estimated in a Round Robin procedure.

5   Probabilistic Modeling

5.1   Introduction

The algorithm is based on a standard probabilistic modeling approach. If D is a dialogue and L is a possible segmentation the Viterbi algorithm is used to find the best segmentation L^*

$$L^* = \text{argmax}_L \ p(L|D) = \text{argmin}_L \ -\log p(\text{S})$$

where $S = \langle D_0, \ldots, D_n \rangle$ is the dialogue segmented into topical segments D_i. The model for $p(S)$ is assumed to be decomposable into models for the number of segments per dialogue $p(\#segments)$, the length of each segment $p(\text{length}(d_i))$ and models for the content of each segment given the segment length $p(d_i|\text{length}(d_i))$:

$$p(s) = p(\#segments) \prod_i p(\text{length}(d_i)) p(d_i|\text{length}(d_i))$$

The most crucial assumption of this model is that all segments are assumed to be independent of each other which is invalid in general, especially when a topic is resumed after a digression. The dialogue segmentation model can be simplified by assuming exponential models for $p(\#segments)$ and $p(\text{length}(d_i))$ and which allows to consolidate the two into a single penalty P in the optimization:

$$L^* = \text{argmin}_L \sum_i P - \log p(d_i | \text{length}(d_i))$$

where d_i is the ith segment of d with respect to the segmentation L. Since the dialogue d is known we may call $d[l : k]$ the segment ranging from k to l and define

$$M_{k,l-k-1} := -\log p(d[k : l] | \text{length}(d[k : l]))$$

Finding the most likely sequence corresponds to finding the best sequence L of strictly ascending indices such that the sequence contains 0 as the first index and size of M as the last:

$$L^* = \text{argmin}_L \sum_{0 < i \leq \text{size}(L)} P + M_{L[i-1], L[i]-L[i-1]-1}$$

Since very long segments are extremely unlikely our implementation uses a maximum length constraint of 300 turns. This number was chosen conservatively such that almost no mistake was made, however the win in runtime was significant since dialogues can be very long. The parameter P may be chosen to derive segmentations of different lengths. Two different strategies are used for determining P for a test utterance, the *penalty criterion* for the C99-database and *segment ratio criterion* the dialogue databases: The *penalty criterion* determines P on the training database by taking the mean of the P_i for each training utterance which generate the correct number of segments for that utterance. The *segment ratio criterion* determines the average number of utterances per topic on the training database which is used to determine the number of topics for a test utterance. P is determined for each test utterance using a logarithmic search such that the desired number of segments is obtained. Training and testing is done in a Round Robin fashion such that the whole database can be tested.

5.2   Coherence Features

Keyword repetition and speaker initiative can both be modeled as coherence features by assuming that each segment follows its own language model. In the case of keyword repetition the language model describes the keywords, for speaker initiative it describes the speaker identity of an utterance and potentially an indication of the initiative such as utterance length (see Sec. 6 for details on the implementation of the features). The probabilistic model requires to define $\log p(d_i | \text{length}(d_i))$ in an appropriate fashion. Speech recognition researchers [12] pioneered the use of so called cache models that adapt themselves over time. Cache models have been used in two flavors in the speech recognition community: Either similar to [12] and accurately following the probabilistic framework

by continuously updating the context and calculating the probability for the
next word on the fly (the dynamic approach) or by recognizing a segment of
speech and training a static language model on the speech recognition result
(the static approach). While initial experiments used both models there are no
differences in the experimental results. Since the static model is simpler to im-
plement and faster in execution it is used for all experiments reported. The static
model approach seems to be somewhat counterintuitive at first but it can also
be explained in the minimum description length framework. The probabilistic
framework can explain the static model by associating a language model with
each segment boundary. The random variable L may be reinterpreted as the
segmentation including the likelihood of the segment language model. If all language models are assumed to be equally likely it is modeled by another penalty
that can be subsumed by P. To obtain better estimates and avoid "zero probabilities" the cache model was smoothed using absolute discounting with a fixed
parameter $D = 0.5$ [22]. The discounting method and parameters used were
fairly uncritical when compared to alternatives during prestudies.

5.3   Region Features

Region features are an extension of the common boundary modeling approach to
discourse segmentation. A region mapping is a function f which maps an integer
k onto an array of k region labels. It can therefore be naturally extended to a
function f' which maps a segment d_i containing k utterances to k segmentation
labels. The intuition is that if the length of the segment is known it has to follow
a certain fixed pattern. The simplest example is the classic *boundary modeling*
approach where

$$f(k)[j] := \begin{cases} \text{BOUNDARY if } j = 0 \\ \text{NONBOUNDARY otherwise} \end{cases}$$

The *boundary modeling* assumes that there are very specific phrase or intona-
tional events at or near the boundary (key words and phrases). The *equal size
regions* approach (3 regions for Begin, Middle and End) can easily model changes
in general distributions such as the part of speech distribution: At the beginning
new items are introduced explicitly whereas they are referred to anaphorically
towards the end. They can be combined in the *equal size + boundary* approach
which features one region for the boundary and Begin, Middle and End regions.
Since f' is a deterministic function of the segment length $\text{length}(d_i)$

$$p(d_i|\text{length}(d_i)) = p(d_i|f'(d_i), \text{length}(d_i))$$

In order to make this quantity tractable independence assumptions have to be
made: All segments in a topic are independent given the segmentation labels,
all segments depend only on their respective segmentation label and after those
assumptions are applied there is no more dependency on the length of the segment:

$$p(d_i|\text{length}(d_i)) = \prod_j \frac{p(f'(d_i)_j|d_{i_j})}{p(f'(d_i)_j)} \cdot \prod_j p(d_{i_j})$$

where $f'(d_i)_j$ is the jth region label of $f'(d_i)$ and d_{i_j} is the jth utterance of the region d_i. Since $p(d_{i_j})$ is independent of the segmentation L it can be ignored in the search procedure. The score of the model is therefore just the probability of the region label given the dialogue segment (as determined by a classifier such as a neural network) divided by the prior of the region label.

The advantage of this approach is that it extends boundary classification to the classification of multiple regions. It is particularly useful if we assume that simple regions of topics have different properties which may provide a natural model of prosodic and stylistic difference across regions. If one would use language model classifiers using part-of-speech as features to determine $\frac{p(f'(d_i)_j|d_{i_j})}{p(f'(d_i)_j)}$ the model would burn down to the training of part-of-speech Markov models for each segment of a topic which provides an intuitive description stylistic regions. Alternatively one could train a classifier with the same parameterization discriminative – a neural network without hidden units and the softmax function as its output or exponential models are such classifiers (see also [29]).

6   Experiments

The experiments were carried out on the CallHome Spanish, a corpus of meetings, the Santa Barbara corpus and a database used by [4] (C99-database). All experiments have been carried out on manual transcripts unless noted otherwise – only for the meeting corpus speech recognition results have been available:

CallHome Spanish. The whole corpus (120 conversations, approximately 20 minutes each) has been hand annotated with topical segmentations. The corpus features telephone calls in Spanish between family members calling from the US to their home countries. The original corpus [15] was published by [17] and recently the topical segmentation along with further dialogue annotation from our project Clarity were published as well [14].

Santa Barbara. 7 of 12 English dialogues [13] have been segmented manually. The corpus features all kinds of oral interactions including meetings, evening events and kitchen table discussions.

Meetings. 8 English dialogues have been annotated with topic segmentation and 2 of those have been processed using a speech recognizer. The meetings are recordings of group meetings, mostly of our own data collection group. The latest published speech recognition error rates for this corpus are around 40% word error rate and the out of vocabulary rate is about 1-2% for each meeting [34,38]. Speech recognition results were available for two out of eight meetings and the topical segmentation has been transferred to those (see Sec. 4).

C99-database [4] used the Brown corpus to generate an artificial topic segmentation problem and the corpus is available (see [4]). A small program randomly grabbed initial portions of Brown corpus texts and concatenated them as the topics of an artificial text. The database consists of four subparts: 100 texts with topics 3-5, 6-8 and 9-11 sentences in length and 400 with topics of 3-11 sentences in length. The "all" database is the concatenation of these four databases. To maintain consistency with his results his formula for the average link error rate has been used.

The first question addressed was whether the probabilistic modeling approach for keyword repetition and speaker initiative compares well to standard algorithms. The stopwords were removed from all databases and the first four letters were retained from each word for all databases. On the C99-database Porter stemming [26] was used instead of the 4 letter stemming. Additionally the corresponding formula for the calculation of the link error rate was used on the C99-database (Sec. 4) to allow comparisons with [4]. For speaker initiative each utterance was replaced by a single token representing the speaker identity and the information whether the speaker turn was long or short (a turn was defined as short if it contains three words or less). In Tab. 1 the probabilistic approach (R01) was compared to [4] (C99) and the texttiling [9] approach (Tile). To present Tile in the best light the implementation provided on Hearst's WWW page was chosen on the dialogue segmentation tasks and the reimplementation of [4] on the C99 database [4].

The results show that the new algorithm delivers excellent results on the dialogue databases: The results are always better than the other algorithms, in some cases by large margins [5]. The only exception is the speaker initiative criterion for the CallHome database which may however be a bad example since speaker initiative is likely a bad criterion for that database (see further discussion below). Tile and C99 seem to perform similar.

The results for the C99 database are very different, the C99 and R01 algorithms perform similar with the exception of the 9-11 part of the database where C99 performs a lot better. The situation changes if the algorithms for determining the number of segments are changed: If the number of segments for R01 is chosen to be the number of C99 the result of R01 is not much worse. If both algorithms are given the number of segments from the reference R01 performs better. As noted above R01 worked a lot better on the C99-database using the *penalty criterion* unlike the *segmentation ratio criterion* used on the dialogue databases. Given these results the author cautions the interpretation of the results on the C99-database since it has been artificially constructed. Specifically the length distribution of the segments seem to be unnatural and may place too much weight on the algorithm determining the number of segments. Overall R01

---

[4] Note that the same stemming algorithms were used for all algorithms – [4] didn't use Porter stemming in the tiling implementation which was used here and Hearst's algorithm was also fed with the exact same input as the others. The author replaced the stopword removal and stemming from the external algorithms and replaced them with his own implementation. The native implementation of the Porter algorithm of C99 delivered identical results to the reimplementation used here.

[5] The results for Tile and C99 improve when their native criterion for determining the number of segments is replaced by the *segmentation ratio* criterion presented here – however R01 still performs significantly better. These results are not shown in the tables since they are secondary and would require much more space.

Table 1. Algorithm comparison: The proposed algorithm (R01) is compared to [4] (C99) and [9] (Tile) for keyword coherence and speaker initiative based topical segmentation. The equal distance baseline (baseline) is listed for comparison. It delivers excellent results on all database slightly worse results than C99 on C99-database. The results on the C99 database however have to be taken with a grain of salt due to the artificial construction of the database.

	Link error rate in %			
Database	R01	C99	Tile	Baseline
Dialogue segmentation, keyword repetition				
SantaBarbara	39.0	53.7	49.2	49.0
CallHome	37.9	40.4	44.1	45.9
Meetings	37.6	45.2	44.6	47.8
Dialogue segmentation, speaker initiative				
SantaBarbara	35.3	41.6	42.3	49.0
CallHome	45.5	43.8	43.0	45.9
Meetings	38.9	39.7	39.7	47.8
C99 database, keyword repetition				
All	13.8	12.8	30.4	42
3-11	13.6	13.0	29.9	45
3-5	17.2	17.7	36.7	38
6-8	8.9	9.6	26.8	39
9-11	16.1	10.0	29.7	36

Table 2. Dialogue segmentation: Topical segmentation was tested on the Santa Barbara corpus, CallHome Spanish and the meeting corpus, all corpora manually transcribed and annotated with speakers. Two types of features are being compared, keyword repetition and speaker repetition.

	Link error rate in %				
Features	None	4 letters	No mapping	Trigram	
Stopwords	No	Yes	No	Yes	Yes
Santa Barbara (baseline 49.0%)					
	39.0	38.6	41.1	41.0	43.8
Speaker + ls	35.3	38.5	38.7	35.9	41.8	41.8
Speaker	39.1	36.4	39.4	36.2	40.5	41.7
CallHome Spanish (baseline 45.9%)					
	38.6	38.4	39.4	38.6	37.2
Speaker + ls	45.6	38.8	39.6	39.3	38.3	37.3
Speaker	45.3	38.4	38.3	39.1	38.8	37.2
Meetings,topic segmented database (8 meetings) manual transcript (baseline 47.8%) Second human 32.3%					
	37.6	33.1	37.6	34.3	35.3
Speaker + ls	38.9	35.6	33.1	36.9	32.9	33.7
Speaker	42.6	36.0	32.9	37.9	33.8	34.9

Table 3. Speech Recognition: Two of the meetings have been fully decoded by an LVCSR system with a word error rate of approximately 40% [34]. The *4 letter* word normalization has been used (see Tab. 2).

Meetings, LVCSR database		
	Link error rate in %	
Features	manual	machine
baseline	42.4	42.1
words,no stopwords	34.3	38.7
words+stopwords	32.5	35.2
speaker+ls	36.9	36.5
speaker+ls and words, no stopwords	34.0	39.4
speaker+ls and words+stopwords	30.4	33.6

is slightly worse than C99 on this database yet much better than Tile and the other algorithms tested in [4].

Tab. 2 compares coherence features. For word repetition the following choices can be made: (a) should stopwords be modeled as well and (b) should a word be mapped onto some baseform (stemming). The inclusion of stopwords may model the speaker identity implicitly or it may model general speaking style. The stemming algorithms tested were *No mapping* which doesn't perform any stemming, the *4-letter* stemming which maps a word onto its first 4 letters and the *trigram* method which maps each word onto the trigrams that occur in it. The *4 letter* stemming seems to be effective. Additional attempts to use Porter stemming [26] on the English database did not show improved results. The *trigram* stemming may capture endearments or other morphological features in Spanish which may explain its effectiveness on CallHome. The inclusion of stop words is typically improving the performance if speaker initiative is not modeled.

For speaker initiative each utterance can either be replaced by the speaker identity itself (*Speaker*) or the speaker identity plus the information whether the utterance was long or short (*Speaker+LS*). An utterance is called short if it contains three words or less. This definition is designed to capture the information whether a speaker issued a dominant dialogue act or a non-dominant dialogue act. Short utterance tend to be non-dominant dialogue acts such as backchannels or answers. A strong correlation of dominance and the dialogue act type has been shown empirically by [16] and the results indicate that the *Speaker+LS* feature performs significantly better than the *Speaker* feature by itself. The long/short criterion has the advantage that it may also be implemented easily without having access to a speech recognition engine. Other encodings of speaker initiative did not improve the results.

The speaker initiative approach doesn't seem to be very successful on Call-Home Spanish. The reason for that fact may be seen in the familiarity of the speakers and their established (dominance) relationship as well as in the fact that one speaker is abroad whereas the other is "back home". Both properties

Table 4. Segmentation using word based regions: A neural network (NN) and language model classifier (LM) were trained to discriminate between different regions of topical segments, either just boundary vs. non-boundary, equal sized regions (begin/middle/end) or a combination of the two (both). The table shows the combination of these features with keyword repetition (keyword) and speaker initiative (speaker+LS) and the combination of the two (both).

Coherence feature	No region	Segmentation					
		boundary		equal size		both	
		NN	LM	NN	LM	NN	LM
CallHome Spanish							
none	45.9	43.4	42.6	38.3	39.3	36.5	37.8
keyword	38.6	35.8	34.1	36.2	35.6	34.7	33.6
speaker+ls	45.6	42.8	42.3	43.2	42.2	41.9	41.4
both	38.8	36.5	34.3	37.4	35.7	35.6	34.9
Meeting							
none	47.8	38.9	37.4	42.1	45.1	41.5	46.0
keyword	37.6	36.2	37.9	37.9	36.9	37.1	39.5
speaker+ls	35.6	38.0	36.7	40.7	36.9	39.7	40.1
both	36.0	37.7	36.1	35.6	36.3	36.6	35.8
Santa Barbara							
none	49.0	40.1	41.0	43.4	48.9	44.1	48.2
keyword	39.0	40.0	38.1	39.7	40.4	39.5	40.8
speaker+ls	38.5	37.7	38.0	38.8	42.9	38.9	41.0
both	36.4	36.2	38.9	37.5	38.7	37.4	37.1

may lead to dialogues where the dominance is rarely shifting between topics. For the multi-party dialogues in the Santa Barbara and meeting corpus however speaker initiative outperforms the keyword based approach. On meetings the combination of the two delivers the best results.

Tab. 3 demonstrates the effect of speech recognition on the segmentation accuracy. While the result for keywords information is worse using speech recognition it is not as bad as one might assume. This result may also be due to consistent misrecognitions that might be produced by a speech recognizer due to keywords that are missing from the vocabulary. Using stopwords additionally to words resulted in a significant improvement in link error rate with no degradation introduced by the speech recognizer. Speaker initiative can be used by itself and it can be combined successfully with word and stopword information. The results have to be taken with caution due to the small size of the database available and the manual annotation of speaker identity.

In Tab. 4 the effect of part-of-speech features for region modeling is shown. A neural network classifier was trained without hidden units, the softmax output function was used as the output function. The vocabulary for the neural network (NN) and language model (LM) classifier were the most frequent 500 word/part of speech pairs while the remaining words are mapped on their part of speech. The effects are clear especially for the equal size+boundary region model and the improvements can also be confirmed when combining the model with repetition modeling, especially on CallHome Spanish. It is therefore clear that there are changes in the word and part of speech distributions in different topical regions. However the combination of word based region modeling with the best repetition model didn't always yield better results for the other databases. Neural network performed significantly better than language models as region classifiers on some segmentation tasks but are slightly worse on some others.

7   Conclusion

A probabilistic framework for dialogue segmentation is presented and applied. The algorithm proposed has a clean probabilistic interpretation and performs well compared to [9,4], especially on dialogue databases. There is still room for improvement, especially information about cooccurrence of words could be included in the model as suggested by [2,25,37] and more work on prosodic features could be attempted. The algorithm was tested on a variety of spontaneous speech corpora and (stemmed) keywords, character n-gram and speaker initiative were used as features. Speaker initiative was found to perform almost as well as keyword repetition: This finding confirms the intuition that topical change is correlated with the activity the speaker are engaging in and their speaking rights which is encoded in their speaker initiative distribution. The results however also show that speaker initiative may fail in certain situations such as CallHome Spanish where only one speaker is dominant while the topic may be changing. Determining speaker initiative according to the definition here should be very tractable since speaker identity may be available trivially or it can be determined very effectively and reliably in meeting situations [23]. Modeling begin/middle/end as well as the boundary of a topical segment it was possible to exploit changes in the word and part of speech distribution.

Dialogue segmentation can therefore be done with a couple of features with similar performance. These features include lexical cohesion, speaker initiative and changes in the part of speech profile. The results presented here therefore fit the general claim of the author that dialogue style has to be an important feature in information access systems for spoken interactions. Speech recognition – even on hard corpora – didn't have a disastrous impact on the segmentation performance but resulted in significant degradation. Speaker initiative is a very powerful criterion which can likely be detected reliably without the need for expensive LVCSR.

References

1. J. Allan, J. Carbonell, G. Doddington, J. P. Yamron, and Y. Yang. Topic detection and tracking pilot study: Final report. In *Proceedings of the DARPA Broadcast News Transcription and Understanding Workshop*, Lansdowne, Virginia, USA, February 1998.

2. D. Beeferman, A. Berger, and J. Lafferty. Statistical models for text segmentation. *Machine Learning*, 34:177–210, 1999. Special Issue on Natural Language Learning (C. Cardie and R. Mooney, eds).
3. J. Carletta, A. Isard, S. Isard, J. C. Kowtko, G. Doherty-Sneddon, and A. H. Anderson. The reliability of a dialogue structure coding scheme. *Computational Linguistics*, 23(1):13–31, March 1997.
4. F. Choi. Advances in domain independent linear text segmentation. In *Proceedings of NAACL*, Seattle, USA, 2000. Available with software at: http://www.cs.man.ac.uk/~choif/ http://xxx.lanl.gov/abs/cs.CL/0003083.
5. J. Garofolo, C. Auzanne, and E. Voorhees. The TREC spoken document retrieval track : A success story. In E. Voorhees, editor, *Text Retrieval Conference (TREC) 8*, Gaithersburg, Maryland, USA, 1999. November 16-19.
6. P. Geutner, M. Finke, and P. Scheytt. Adaptive vocabularies for transcribing multilingual broadcast news. In *ICASSP*, 1998.
7. B. Grosz and C. Sidner. Attention, intention and the structure of discourse. *Computational Linguistics*, 12(3):172–204, 1986.
8. M. Halliday and R. Hasan. *Cohesion in English*. Longman Group, 1976.
9. M. A. Hearst. Texttiling: Segmenting text into multi-paragraph subtopic passages. *Computational Linguistics*, 23(1):33–64, March 1997.
10. J. Hirschberg and C. Nakatani. Acoustic indicators of topic segmentation. In *ICSLP*, Sidney, Australia, 1998.
11. M.-Y. Kan, J. Klavans, and K. R. McKeown. Linear segmentation and segment significance. In *Proceedings of the 6th International Workshop on Very Large Corpora (WVLC-6)*, pages 197–205, Montreal, Canada, August 1998.
12. R. Kuhn and R. de Mori. A cache-base natural language model for speech recognition. *IEEE Transactions on Pattern Analysis and machince Intelligence*, 12(6):570–583, June 1990.
13. Santa barbara corpus of spoken american english part-i, 2000.
14. Callhome spanish dialogue act annotation, 2001. catalogue number LDC2001T61.
15. Callhome spanish, lexicon, speech and transcripts, 1996. catalogue number LDC96L16, LDC96S35 catalogue number LDC96L16, LDC96S35 .
16. P. Linell, L. Gustavsson, and P. Juvonen. Interactional dominance in dyadic communication: a presentation of initiative-response analysis. *Linguistics*, 26:415–442, 1988.
17. Linguistic Data Consortium (LDC). Catalogue, 2000. http://www.ldc.upenn.edu/.
18. W. C. Mann and S. Thomson. Rhetorical structure theory: Towards a functional theory of text organization. *TEXT*, 8:243–281, 1988.
19. D. Marcu. *The Rhetorical Parsing, Summarization, and Generation of Natural Language Texts*. PhD thesis, Department of Computer Science, University of Toronto, December 1997. Also published as Technical Report CSRG-371, Computer Systems Research Group, University of Toronto.
20. E. Mittendorf and P. Schäuble. Document and passage retrieval based on hidden markov models. In *Proceedings of the Seventeenth Annual International ACM SIGIR Conference on Research and Development in Information Retrieval*, Dublin, Ireland, 1994.
21. T. P. Moran, L. Palen, S. Harrison, P. Chiu, D. Kimber, S. Minneman, W. van Melle, and P. Zellweger. "i'll get that off the audio": A case study of salvaging multimedia meeting records. In *CHI 97*, 1997.
22. H. Ney, U. Essen, and R. Kneser. On structuring probabilistic dependencies in stochastic language modeling. *Computer Speech and Language*, 8:1–35, 1994.

23. Y. Pan and A. Waibel. The effects of room acoustics on MFCC speech parameters. In *Proceedings of the ICSLP*, Beijing, China, 2000.
24. R. J. Passonneau and D. J. Litman. Discourse segmentation by human and automated means. *Computational Linguistics*, 23(1):103, March 1997. 139.
25. J. M. Ponte and B. W. Croft. Text segmentation by topic. In *Proceedings of the first European Conference on research and advanced technology for digital libraries*, 1997. U.Mass. Computer Science Technical Report TR97-18.
26. M. Porter. An algorithm for suffix stripping. *Program*, 14(3):130–137, July 1980.
27. F. Quek, D. McNeill, R. Bryll, C. Kirbas, H. Arslan, K. E. McCullough, and N. Furuyama. Gesture, speech, and gaze cues for discourse segmentation. In *Proceedings of the Computer Vision and Pattern Recognition CVPR*, 2000.
28. J. C. Reynar. *Topic segmentation: Algorithms and applications.* PhD thesis, Computer and Information Science, University of Pennsylvenia, 1998. Institute for Research in Cognitive Science (IRCS), University of Pennsylvenia, Technical report: IRCS-98-21.
29. K. Ries. HMM and neural network based speech act classification. In *Proceedings of the IEEE Conference on Acoustics, Speech, and Signal Processing*, volume 1, pages 497–500, Phoenix, AZ, March 1999.
30. K. Ries, L. Levin, L. Valle, A. Lavie, and A. Waibel. Shallow discourse genre annotation in callhome spanish. In *Proceecings of the International Conference on Language Ressources and Evaluation (LREC-2000)*, Athens, Greece, May 2000.
31. K. Ries and A. Waibel. Activity detection for information access to oral communication. In *Human Language Technology Conference*, Sand Diego, CA, USA, March 2001.
32. E. Shriberg, A. Stolcke, D. Hakkani-Tür, and G. Tür. Prosody modeling for automatic sentence and topic segmentation from speech. *Speech Communication*, 32(1-2):127–154, 2000. Special Issue on Accessing Information in Spoken Audio.
33. A. Singhal and F. Pereira. Document expansion for speech retrieval. In *In Proceedings of SIGIR*, 1999.
34. A. Waibel, M. Bett, F. Metze, K. Ries, T. Schaaf, T. Schultz, H. Soltau, H. Yu, and K. Zechner. Advances in automatic meeting record creation and access. In *ICASSP*, Salt Lake City, Utah, USA, 2001.
35. M. A. Walker and S. Whittaker. Mixed initiative in dialogue: An investigation into discourse segmentation. In *In Proc. 28th Annual Meeting of the ACL*, 1990.
36. S. Whittaker, P. Hyland, and M. Wiley. Filochat: handwritten notes provide access to recorded conversations. In *In Proceedings of CHI94 Conference on Computer Human Interaction*, pages 271–277, 1994.
37. Yamron, I. Carp, L. Gillick, S. Lowe, and P. van Mulbregt. A hidden markov model approach to text segmentation and event tracking. In *Proceedings of ICASSP*, volume 1, pages 333–336, Seattle, WA, May 1998.
38. H. Yu, T. Tomokiyo, Z. Wang, and A. Waibel. New developments in automatic meeting transcription. In *Proceedings of the ICSLP*, Beijing, China, October 2000.
39. K. Zechner and A. Waibel. DIASUMM: Flexible summarization of spontaneous dialogues in unrestricted domains. In *Proceedings of COLING*, Saarbrücken, Germany, 2000.

Extracting Caller Information from Voicemail

Jing Huang, Geoffrey Zweig, and Mukund Padmanabhan

IBM T. J. Watson Research Center
Yorktown Heights, NY 10598
{jhuang, gzweig, mukund}@watson.ibm.com

Abstract. In this paper we address the problem of extracting caller information from voicemail messages, such as the identity and phone number of the caller. Previous work in information extraction from speech includes spoken document retrieval and named entity detection. This task differs from the named entity task in that the information we are interested in is a subset of the named entities in the message, and consequently, the need to pick the correct subset makes the problem more difficult. Also, the caller's identity may include information that is not typically associated with a named entity. In this work, we present two information extraction methods, one based on hand-crafted rules, one based on statistically trained maximum entropy model. We evaluate their performance on both manually transcribed messages and on the output of a speech recognition system.

1 Introduction

In recent years, the task of automatically extracting information from data has grown in importance, as a result of an increase in the number of publicly available archives and a realization of the commercial value of the available data. One aspect of information extraction (IE) is the retrieval of documents. Another aspect is that of identifying words from a stream of text that belong in pre-defined categories, for instance, "named entities" such as proper names, organizations, or numerics. Though most of the earlier IE work was done in the context of text sources, recently a great deal of work has also focused on extracting information from speech sources. Examples of this are the Spoken Document Retrieval (SDR) task [1], named entity (NE) extraction [2,3,4]. The SDR task focused on Broadcast News and the NE task focused on both Broadcast News and telephone conversations.

In this paper, we focus on a source of conversational speech data, voicemail, that is found in relatively large volumes in the real-world, and that could benefit greatly from the use of IE techniques. The goal here is to query one's personal voicemail for items of information, without having to listen to the entire message. For instance, "who called today?", or "what is X's phone number?". Because of the importance of these key pieces of information, in this paper, we focus precisely on extracting the identity and the phone number of the caller. Other attempts at summarizing voicemail have been made in the past [5], however the

A.R. Coden, E.W. Brown, and S. Srinivasan (Eds.): IR Techniques ..., LNCS 2273, pp. 67–77, 2002.
© Springer-Verlag Berlin Heidelberg 2002

goal there was to compress a voicemail message by summarizing it, and not to extract the answers to specific questions.

An interesting aspect of this research is that because a transcription of the voicemail is not available, automatic speech recognition (ASR) algorithms have to be used to convert the speech to text and the subsequent IE algorithms must operate on the transcription. One of the complications that we have to deal with is the fact that the state-of-the-art accuracy of speech recognition algorithms on this type of data is only in the neighborhood of 60-70% [6]. The large word error rate is due to the fact that the speech is spontaneous, and characterized by poor grammar, false starts, pauses, hesitations, etc. While this does not pose a problem for a human listener, it causes significant problems for speech recognition algorithms.

The task that is most similar to our work is named entity extraction from speech data [2]. Although the goal of the named entity task is similar - to identify the names of persons, locations, organizations, and temporal and numeric expressions - our task is different, and in some ways more difficult. There are two main reasons for this: first, caller and number information constitute a small fraction of all named entities. Not all person-names belong to callers, and not all digit strings specify phone-numbers. In this sense, the algorithms we use must be more precise than those for named entity detection. Second, the caller's identity may include information that is not typically found in a named entity, for example, "Joe on the third floor", rather than simply "Joe". We discuss our definitions of "caller" and "number" in Section 2.

To extract caller information from transcribed speech text, we implemented two different systems, both statistical and non-statistical approaches. We evaluate these systems on manual voicemail transcriptions as well as the output of a speech recognizer. The first system is a simple rule-based system that uses trigger phrases to identify the information-bearing words. The second system is a maximum entropy model that tags the words in the transcription as belonging to one of the categories, "caller's identity", "phone number" or "other".

The rest of the paper is organized as follows: Section 2 describes the database we are using; Section 3 contains a description of the baseline system; Section 4 describes the maximum entropy model and the associated features; Section 5 contains our experimental results and Section 6 concludes our discussions.

2   Database

Our work focuses on a database of voicemail messages gathered at IBM, and made publicly available through the LDC. This database and related speech recognition work is described fully in [6]. We worked with approximately 5,000 messages, which we divided into 3,700 messages for training, 500 for development test set, and 800 for evaluation test set. The messages were manually transcribed with about 3% errors and then a human tagger identified the portions of each message that specified the caller and any return numbers that were left. In this work, we take a broad view of what constitutes a caller or number. The caller was defined to be the consecutive sequence of words that best answered the question "who called?". The definition of a number we used is a sequence of consecutive words that enables a return call to be placed. Thus, for example, a caller might be "Angela *from P.C. Labs*," or "Peggy Cole *Reed Balla's secretary*". Similarly, a number may not be a digit string, for example: "*tieline* eight oh five six," or "*pager* one three five". No more than one caller was identified for a single message, though there could be multiple numbers. The training of the maximum entropy model and statistical transducer are done on these annotated scripts.

3   Rule-Based Baseline System

In voicemail messages, people often identify themselves and give their phone numbers in highly stereotyped ways. So for example, someone might say, "Hi Joe it's Harry..." or "Give me a call back at extension one one eight four." Our baseline system takes advantage of this fact by enumerating a set of transduction rules - in the form of a *flex* program - that transduce out the key information in a call.

The baseline system is built around the notion of "trigger phrases". These hand-crafted phases are patterns that are used in the flex program to recognize caller's identity and phone numbers. Examples of trigger phrases are "Hi this is", and "Give me a call back at". In order to identify names and phone numbers as generally as possible, our baseline system has defined classes for person-names and numbers.

In addition to trigger phrases, "trigger suffixes" proved to be useful for identifying phone numbers. For example, the phrase "thanks bye" frequently occurs immediately after the caller's phone number. In general, a random sequence of digits cannot be labeled as a phone number; but, a sequence of digits followed by "thanks bye" is almost certainly the caller's phone number. So when the flex program matches a sequence of digits, it stores it; then it tries to match a trigger suffix. If this is successful, the digit string is recognized a phone number string. Otherwise the digit string is ignored.

Our baseline system has about 200 rules. Its creation was aided by an automatically generated list of short, commonly occurring phrases that were then manually scanned and added to the flex program. It is the simplest of the systems presented, and achieves a good performance level (see Table 3), but suffers from the fact that a skilled person is required to identify the rules.

4   Maximum Entropy Model

Maximum entropy modeling is a powerful framework for constructing statistical models from data. It has been used in a variety of difficult classification tasks such as part-of-speech tagging [7], prepositional phrase attachment [8] and named entity tagging [9], and achieves state of the art performance. In the following, we briefly describe the application of these models to extracting caller's information from voicemail messages.

The problem of extracting the information pertaining to the callers identity and phone number can be thought of as a tagging problem, where the tags are "caller's identity," "caller's phone number" and "other." The objective is to tag each word in a message into one of these categories. Further, in order to segment repeated patterns, for each tag t there are two sub-tags: $begin\_t$ and t. For example, "*hi jim this is patricia at bank united ... call me back at two nine two three*" would be tagged as "*other other other other begin_caller caller caller caller ... other other other other begin_number number number number*".

The information that can be used to predict the tag of a word is the context of its surrounding words and their associated tags. Let $\mathcal{H}$ denote the set of possible word and tag contexts, called "*histories*", and $\mathcal{T}$ denote the set of tags. The maxent model is then defined over $\mathcal{H} \times \mathcal{T}$, and predicts the conditional probability $p(t|h)$ for a tag t given the history h. The computation of this probability depends on a set of binary-valued "features" $f_i(h, t)$.

Given some training data and a set of features the maximum entropy estimation procedure computes a weight parameter α_i for every feature f_i and parameterizes $p(t|h)$ as follows:

$$p(t|h) = \frac{\prod_i \alpha_i^{f_i(h,t)}}{Z} \tag{1}$$

where Z is a normalization constant.

The role of the features is to enumerate co-occurrences of histories and tags, and find histories that are strong predictors of specific tags. (for example, the tag "begin_caller" is very often preceded by the word sequence "this is"). If a feature is a very strong predictor of a particular tag, then the corresponding α_i would be high. It is also possible that a particular feature may be a strong predictor of the absence of a particular tag, in which case the associated α_i would be near zero.

Training a maximum entropy model involves the selection of the features and the subsequent estimation of weight parameters α_i. The testing procedure involves a search to enumerate the candidate tag sequences for a message and choosing the one with highest probability. We use the "beam search" technique of [7] to search the space of all hypotheses.

4.1   Features

Designing effective features is crucial to the maxent model. In the following sections, we describe the various feature functions that we experimented with. We first preprocess the text in the following ways: (1) map rare words (with counts less than 5) to a fixed word "UNKNOWN"; (2) map words in a name dictionary to a fixed word "NAME" (which is called meta-name). The first step is a way to handle out of vocabulary words in test data; the second step takes advantage of known names. This mapping makes the model focus on learning features which help to predict the location of the caller identity and leave the actual specific names later for extraction.

Unigram Lexical Features. To compute unigram lexical features, we used the neighboring two words, and the tags associated with the previous two words to define the history h_i as

$$h_i = w_i, w_{i+1}, w_{i+2}, w_{i-1}, w_{i-2}, t_{i-1}, t_{i-2} \qquad (2)$$

The features are generated by scanning each pair (h_i, t_i) in the training data with feature template in Table 1, where X denotes an instance of a word, T, T_1, T_2 are values of t_i, t_{i-1}, t_{i-2}.

Table 1. Unigram features of the current history h_i.

	Features	
$\forall w_i$	$w_i = X$	$\& \; t_i = T$
	$t_{i-1} = T_1$	$\& \; t_i = T$
	$t_{i-2}t_{i-1} = T_2T_1$	$\& \; t_i = T$
	$w_{i-1} = X$	$\& \; t_i = T$
	$w_{i-2} = X$	$\& \; t_i = T$
	$w_{i+1} = X$	$\& \; t_i = T$
	$w_{i+2} = X$	$\& \; t_i = T$

Bigram Lexical Features. The trigger phrases used in the rule-based approach generally comprise of several words, and turn out to be good predictors of the tags. In order to incorporate this information in the maximum entropy framework, we decided to use ngrams that occur in the surrounding word context to generate features. Due to data sparsity and computational cost, we restricted ourselves to using only bigrams. The bigram feature template is shown in Table 2, where X or Y denotes an instance of a word, T, T_1, T_2 are values of t_i, t_{i-1}, t_{i-2}.

Table 2. Bigram features of the current history h_i.

	Features	
$\forall w_i$	$w_i = X$	$\& \; t_i = T$
	$t_{i-1} = T_1$	$\& \; t_i = T$
	$t_{i-2}t_{i-1} = T_2T_1$	$\& \; t_i = T$
	$w_{i-2}w_{i-1} = XY$	$\& \; t_i = T$
	$w_{i-1}w_i = XY$	$\& \; t_i = T$
	$w_i w_{i+1} = XY$	$\& \; t_i = T$
	$w_{i+1}w_{i+2} = XY$	$\& \; t_i = T$

Dictionary Features. First, a number dictionary is used to scan the training data and generate a code for each word which represents "number" or "other". Second, a multi-word dictionary is used to match known pre-caller trigger prefixes and after-phone-number trigger suffixes. The same code is assigned to each word in the matched string as either "pre-caller" or "after-phone-number". The combined stream of codes is added to the history h_i and used to generate features the same way the word sequence are used to generate lexical features.

Learning from Errors. We use the current maximum entropy model to decode the training data. Adding the decoded tags as another stream of data to the history h_i and generating new features, we can train a new model which hopefully learns to correct some errors that the old model makes. We can even add a stream of tags which come from an external system, for example the baseline system, to our maxent model. The maxent model can selectively correct the weakness of the baseline to some extent.

4.2   Feature Selection

Features can be selected by a simple feature count cutoff method. We ignore features whose counts are less than 10. This method results about $10,000$ number of features. To remove irrelevant and redundant features, we experimented with an incremental feature selection scheme: start with uniform distribution $p(t|h)$, no features, at every iteration add a batch of features to the existing set of features, update the model and re-estimate its parameters, and compute the loglikelihood of the training data. The procedure stops when the gain in likelihood becomes small. We also used a cross validation set to avoid over-training.

5   Experimental Results

To evaluate the performance of different systems, we use the conventional *precision P, recall R* and their *F-measure F*, where $P =$ (number of correctly retrieved info) / (number of retrieved info), $R =$ (number of correctly retrieved info) / (total number of correct info in the data set), F is the harmonic mean of P and R: $F = 2 \times P \times R/(P + R)$.

Significantly, we insist on **exact** matches for an answer to be counted as *correct*. The reason for this is that any error is liable to render the information useless, or detrimental. For example, an incorrect phone number can result in unwanted phone charges, and unpleasant conversations. This is different from typical named entity evaluation, where partial matches are given partial credit. Therefore, it should be understood that the precision and recall rates computed with this strict criterion *cannot* be compared to those from named entity detection tasks.

A summary of our results is presented in Tables 3 and 4. Table 3 presents precision and recall rates when manual word transcriptions are used; Table 4 presents these numbers when speech recognition transcripts are used. On the heading line, P refers to precision, R to recall, F to F-measure, C to caller-identity, and N to phone number. Thus P/C denotes "precision on caller identity".

Table 3. Precision and recall rates for different systems on manual transcriptions of voicemail

	P/C	R/C	F/C	P/N	R/N	F/N
baseline	72.9	67.8	70.3	81.1	83.3	82.2
ME1-U	87.9	75.3	81.1	90.2	77.8	83.5
ME1-B	88.8	79.8	84.1	88.1	78.1	82.8
ME2-U-f1	87.9	75.8	81.4	89.7	82.3	85.8
ME2-U-f1-L	88.2	76.1	81.7	90.0	85.9	87.9
ME2-U-f12	87.3	77.6	82.2	89.5	82.7	86.0
ME2-B-f12	88.3	80.0	83.9	89.3	82.7	85.9
ME2-U-f12-I	86.9	77.5	81.9	88.8	81.2	84.8
ME2-B-f12-I	87.0	78.9	82.8	90.3	82.4	86.2

Table 4. Precision and recall rates for different systems on ASR transcriptions of voicemail

	P/C	R/C	F/C	P/N	R/N	F/N
baseline	21.7	17.2	19.2	52.3	53.8	53.0
ME2-U-f1	23.5	15.6	18.8	56.0	51.5	53.7

In these tables, the maximum entropy model is referred to as ME. ME1-U uses unigram lexical features only; ME1-B uses bigram lexical features only. Compared to ME1-U, ME1-B improves recall of caller by 4.5%, but degrades the precision of numbers by 2%. Overall ME1-B performs better than ME1-U with more than double number of features of ME1-U.

ME2-U-f1 uses unigram lexical features and number dictionary features. It improves the recall of phone number by 4.5% upon ME1-U. The number dictionary features really helps retrieving phone numbers; ME2-U-f1-L learns the errors from ME2-U-f1 and improves the performance of both caller and phone numbers as expected; ME2-U-f12 adds the trigger phrase dictionary features to ME2-U-f1. It improves the recall of caller and phone numbers but degrades on the precision of both. Overall it improves a little on the F-measure. ME2-B-f12 uses bigram lexical features, number dictionary features and trigger phrase dictionary features. It has the best recall of caller, again with over two times number of features of ME2-U-f12.

The above variants of ME features are chosen using simple count cutoff method. When the incremental feature selection is used, ME2-U-f12-I reduces the number of features from 9747 to 910 with minor performance loss; ME2-B-f12-I reduces the number of features from 25800 to 2125 with minor performance loss. This results show that the main power of the maxent model comes from a small portion of features while the rest of the features contribute only a little to the model. If memory and speed are of concern, the incremental feature selection is preferable.

There are several observations that can be made from these results. First, the maximum entropy approach has the better performance in terms of precision, and the best recall for the caller's identity compared to the baseline hand-crafted rules. We believe this is because the baseline has an imperfect set of rules for determining the end of a "caller identity" description. On the other hand, the baseline system has higher recall for phone numbers. The runtime for the baseline is real-time because it only needs to scan the message once; the runtime for the maximum entropy model decoding (i.e. beam search) is also fast, 0.05 CPU second for a 40-word long message.

Second there is a significant difference in performance between manual and decoded transcriptions. As expected, the precision and recall numbers are worse in the presence of transcription errors (see Table 4). For example, we present a manual and ASR transcription for a typical voicemail message below. The extracted caller and phone number info are italic words. Because of transcription errors in the ASR output, the caller info in the decoded text is wrong.

Manual:

michael this is *jack folger in dallas we're a reseller of viavoice i'd talked to you about some of the aspects of the program the other day please call me two one four five two eight three thousand soon as you could please thank you*

ASR:

michael this is *jack for something else with the resell or of via voice talk to you about some aztec sanproni please call me at two one four five two eight three thousand cd*

Here is another example where ASR error causes the extracted phone number in the decoded text to be wrong—with an extra "one".

Manual:

i'm calling from barnett if you could please return my call my number's *one eight hundred eight five four five four seven nine and i'll be here until eight forty five tonight thank you*

ASR:

calling from cornet if you could please return my call my number's *one eight hundred eight five four one five four seven nine and i'm here at five forty five to five thanks*

The degradation due to transcription errors could be caused by: (i) words in the context surrounding the names and numbers being corrupted; or (ii) the information itself being corrupted. To investigate this, we did the following experiment: we replaced the regions of decoded text that correspond to the correct caller identity and phone number with the correct manual transcription, and re-did the test.

The results are shown in Table 5. Compared to the results on the manual transcription, the recall numbers for the maximum-entropy tagger are just slightly $(2 - 3\%)$ worse. The precision of the maximum entropy system is still as good as 83%. This indicates that the corruption of the information content due to transcription errors is much more important than the corruption of the context. If measured by the string error rate, none of our systems can be used to extract exact caller and phone number information directly from decoded voicemail; however, the maximum entropy system can be used to locate the information in the message and highlight those positions. Users then can just listen to these portion to get answers without going through the entire message.

Table 5. Precision and recall rates for different systems on replaced ASR transcriptions of voicemail

	P/C	R/C	F/C	P/N	R/N	F/N
baseline	66.3	66.0	66.1	70.8	71.9	71.3
ME2-U-f1	82.8	72.1	77.1	84.4	81.3	82.8

If one listens to the extracted information segments, how much true information will be obtained? We can use alignments to measure how much information in the extracted portion from decoded scripts is correct by doing the following: first compute time intervals (T_d) of the extracted info in the decoded scripts; second compute time intervals (T_r) of the true info in the reference scripts; finally compute interval overlaps of T_d, T_r. Here we redefine Precision = overlaps/total_decoded, and Recall = overlaps/total_reference. Table 6 shows the results: 80% F-measure on phone number, but only 50% F-measure on caller which still needs further improvement.

All the above ME models were trained from reference scripts, because it is easy for a human tagger to identify caller information from reference scripts. Since our goal is to extract caller information directly from the ASR output, it might be better to train the maximum entropy model from the ASR transcriptions with context and features coming directly from decoded text. To do this, we used an alignment between reference scripts and the decoded scripts to automatically tag caller information in decoded scripts. The same ME2-U-f1(D) model was trained from these training messages [1]. The precision and recall

---

[1] Because of missing alignments, only 3000 training messages are used for ME2-U-f1(D) model training.

of this model are shown in Table 6. Compared to the ME2-U-f1 model trained from reference scripts, ME2-U-f1(D) improves everything but the recall of phone numbers. This may be due to the fact of insufficient training data. Once we have more decoded training data for the maximum entropy model, we expect the performance will improve.

Table 6. Precision and recall of time-overlap for different systems on ASR transcriptions of voicemail, where ME2-U-f1(D) was trained from ASR transcriptions

	P/C	R/C	F/C	P/N	R/N	F/N
baseline	77.0	36.0	49.1	84.8	76.2	80.3
ME2-U-f1	73.2	40.5	52.2	84.6	78.6	81.5
ME2-U-f1(D)	78.2	43.1	55.6	86.1	66.0	74.7

6   Conclusion

In this paper, we study how to extract caller information from voicemail messages. The caller info is useful for voicemail indexing and retrieval. In contrast to traditional named entity tasks, we are interested in identifying just a selected subset of the named entities that occur. We implemented and tested manual rule-based system and a statistical tagger on manual transcriptions and transcriptions generated by a speech recognition system. For a baseline, we used a *flex* program with a set of hand-specified information extraction rules. A maximum entropy tagger is compared to the baseline. Both the baseline and the maximum entropy model performed well on manually transcribed messages. They all degraded significantly with 35% speech recognition error. We expect to have more training data for training the maximum entropy tagger, and training the tagger on the decoded transcripts as well. We will also focus on combining the speech recognizer and information extraction in an integrated framework.

References

1. NIST: Proceedings of the Eighth Text REtrieval Conference (TREC-8) (1999)
2. DARPA: Proceedings of the DARPA Broadcast News Workshop (1999)
3. Miller D., Boisen S., Schwartz R., Stone R., Weischedel R.: Named Entity Extraction from Noisy Input: Speech and OCR. Proceedings of ANLP-NAACL (2000) 316–324
4. Kim J.-H., Woodland P.C.: A Rule-based Named Entity Recognition System for Speech Input. Sixth International Conference on Spoken Language Processing (2000)
5. Koumpis K., Renals S.: Transcription and Summarization of Voicemail Speech. Sixth International Conference on Spoken Language Processing (2000)

6. Huang J., Kingsbury B., Mangu L., Padmanabhan M., Saon G., Zweig G.: Recent Improvements in Speech Recognition Performance on Large Vocabulary Conversational Speech (Voicemail and Switchboard). Sixth International Conference on Spoken Language Processing (2000)
7. Ratnaparkhi A.: A Maximum Entropy Part of Speech Tagger: In Brill E., Church K. (eds.) Conference on Empirical Methods in Natural Language Processing (1996)
8. Ratnaparkhi A., Reynar J., Roukos S.: A Maximum Entropy Model for Prepositional Phrase Attachment. Proceedings of the Human Language Technology Workshop (1994) 250–255
9. Andrew Borthwick, John Sterling, Eugene Agichtein, and Ralph Grishman. NYU: Description of the MENE Named Entity System as Used in MUC-7. Seventh Message Understanding Conference(MUC-7) (1998)

Speech and Hand Transcribed Retrieval

Mark Sanderson and Xiao Mang Shou

Department of Information Studies
University of Sheffield
Western Bank, Sheffield, S10 2TN, UK
+44 114 22 22648
{m.sanderson, x.m.shou}@shef.ac.uk

Abstract. This paper describes the issues and preliminary work involved in the creation of an information retrieval system that will manage the retrieval from collections composed of both speech recognised and ordinary text documents. In previous work, it has been shown that because of recognition errors, ordinary documents are generally retrieved in preference to recognised ones. Means of correcting or eliminating the observed bias is the subject of this paper. Initial ideas and some preliminary results are presented.

1   Introduction

At present, the main stream of information retrieval research remains in searching homogenous data collections. However, with the progress of multimedia technologies, the trend for searching heterogeneous data collections is growing. The MIND (Multimedia International Digital Libraries) project [1] that the authors are currently working with provides a typical example for this case. The research in MIND addresses issues that arise when people have remote access to a great many heterogeneous and distributed multimedia digital libraries containing text, images, and audio data such as speech recognised documents. In order to cope effectively with such masses of knowledge, a subset of the digital libraries that most likely contains relevant documents must be identified, selected, and searched. The results obtained from those resources need to be fused and merged into a single result. Both the means of resource selection and data fusion must be achieved without bias.

When ranking documents in a collection in relation to a query, almost all of the weighting schemes and retrieval models used assume that documents are created equal. The presence or absence of a query word or the number of times that a word occurs within documents is assumed to have the same significance across the collection (once document length has been taken into account). If, however, a collection is composed of documents created in different ways, such as a collection of ordinary and speech recognised documents, or collections of speech recognised documents where the recognition accuracy varies widely, the assumptions are likely to be false.

In general, retrieval of the transcripts of spoken documents is viewed as a success [2]; speech recognition (SR) systems are accurate enough to allow retrieval to operate at an acceptable level. Spoken document retrieval (SDR) is being used: internally

A.R. Coden, E.W. Brown, and S. Srinivasan (Eds.): IR Techniques ..., LNCS 2273, pp. 78-85, 2002.

within corporations [3], [4], [5], and as a Web search engine [6], [7], [8]. Word error rates (WER) on the audio documents being retrieved are still relatively high, however, because relevant documents generally contain each query term with a high term frequency (tf), as long as a few of the term occurrences are recognised, relevant documents will be retrieved. If, however, the collection is composed of both speech recognised and ordinary text documents, because the tf of query words in the recognised documents is lower, the ordinary documents will be retrieved in preference to the recognised (see Past Work below). This problem is also found within the collection of spoken documents, some audio documents are likely to be recognised more accurately than others, those recognised well will contain query terms with higher tf than those recognised badly.[1]

Within the framework of the MIND project, it is also assumed that remote digital library providers will be either uninterested or unwilling to provide detailed data on the content of their libraries or the quality of their SRs, therefore, it is desirable to determine the information independently. This paper proposes an approach for dealing with this problem (for speech data) through the automatic identification of spoken documents and subsequent estimation of the word error rate within those documents. Once such information has been gained, document retrieval scores will be adjusted to ensure a fairer ranking. The rest of this paper describes past work in this area, followed by a description of the methods to be used in the system. Some preliminary work is then outlined before finally concluding.

2   Past Work

Although a great deal of research has been conducted in the retrieval of corrupted data, be it scanned text [11], speech [2], [3], or translated foreign language documents [12], relatively little work has investigated the notion of varying levels of corruption in the collection(s) being retrieved. This is perhaps surprising, as it is quite reasonable to expect such variation. Sanderson and Crestani briefly addressed the problem of retrieving from a collection composed of both ordinary and spoken documents [13], reporting that using a conventional $tf \cdot idf$ weighting scheme, ordinary documents were retrieved in preference to spoken documents. Since then, research in the area has come from the Cross Language Information Retrieval (CLIR) community where retrieval from collections composed of documents written in different languages requires consideration of translation accuracy. Poorly translated documents are less likely to be retrieved. Effective methods to deal with this situation have been devised by identifying the language of the documents and biasing ranking algorithms based on training data derived from cross language test collections [12]. Reported as being effective, the only problem with this technique is the assumption that corruption from translation error is consistent across documents of the same language, an assumption that is likely to be false with the corruption from recognition used in MIND.

---

[1] For such documents, there is also the problem of no query term occurrences being recognised at all. Clearly an important problem, which has been addressed in past work (e.g. the document expansion of Singhal [9] and use of multiple hypotheses by Siegler [10]), it is not discussed here.

3   Methods

The proposed means of providing a fair ranking when dealing with collections of documents composed of either ordinary and spoken documents or spoken document recognised at varying levels of accuracy requires two components: a spoken document identification system; and a method to estimate word error rates. They are described here; alternative approaches to providing fair ranking are described in Conclusions and Future work.

3.1   Spoken Document Identification

When considering how to spot if a piece of text was written or automatically recognised, one can view spoken document identification as a form of language identification [14], [15], which is used to identify the kind of language that a given document was written in. Though techniques applied in language identification such as training a word or character based n-gram model for recognised output and ordinary text, etc. could also be used, some surface cues in the document are likely to be able to identify whether or not it is the output of speech recognition. For example, speech recognisers generally do not insert punctuation in a fine granularity level and do not have clear boundary between sentences and paragraphs (here only the raw speech recognised data with no human corrections is considered). Therefore, by examining the ratio of punctuation to non-punctuation tokens, and/or the ratio of capitalised to non-capitalised letters may provide sufficient clues for the identification task. Another possible solution could be to check whether a document contains common spelling mistakes as speech recognisers working from a pre-defined vocabulary do not misspell words. Alternatively, a more sophisticated approach is to determine if the document contains any words that are outside the recogniser's lexicon. However, since different speech recognisers have different lexicons and getting the lexicons of them can be difficult, this method cannot be generally applied.

Table 1 shows some preliminary results by comparing the punctuation and upper case words in 160Mb speech recognised files, 8.5Mb hand transcribed files from TREC-9 collections, four years Financial Times articles from 1991 to 1994 used as ordinary text files and 2Gb HTML files from TREC-8 collections.

From the table, it shows almost an order of magnitude difference in the percentage of punctuation in speech recognised and hand transcribed collections. The punctuation within speech documents contain full stops and apostrophe marks only whereas hand transcriptions contains evenly distributed comma, hyphen, parenthesis and question marks as well as full stops and apostrophes. By further examining the speech recognised documents, most of the full stops are not addressed to finish a sentence but used as abbreviations such as H.I.V., U.N., etc. Though strictly they should not be counted as full stops, the magnitude difference in the punctuation percentage is not affected by including them. The reason that hand transcriptions and HTML files have higher ration of punctuation is that those files tend to use short statements more frequently than formally written newspaper articles.

Table 1. Comparison of punctuation and upper case words in speech recognised, hand transcribed, ordinary and HTML files

	Total words	Total punctuation	Punctuation ratio	Total Capital words	Capital words ratio
Speech recognised	9,117,820	360,359	0.04	9,117,820	1.00
Hand transcribed	822,760	198,151	0.24	59,401	0.07
Ordinary text	87,377,924	14,278,987	0.16	14,392,058	0.16
HTML files	260,863,739	59,213,771	0.23	45,424,755	0.17

The speech recognised documents used in the experiment are the ".srt" format files where all words are in capital letters. This may not always be true as some other speech recognised files may contain lower case letters only. Therefore, our experiment does not cover all situations but extremely high or low rate of upper case words can be used as an indication for speech document identification.

Based on the above experiment result, a further experiment was conducted by setting the threshold of ratio of punctuation to be 0.1 and ration of upper case words to be 0.001. If a document has the percentage of punctuation less than 0.1 and percentage of capital letters less than 0.001, then the document is identified as a speech recognized one. Here a word composes of all capital letters will not be counted in the ratio of upper case words, so the ratio of upper case words in ".srt" format files is converted to be 0.0 in this experiment. The threshold 0.001 was chosen for upper case words because it was found that some HTML files with long listings can have very low ratio of upper case words. All together 348Mb speech recognized files, over 2Gb newspaper articles and 2Gb html files from TREC-8 collections were used in the experiment and the identification accuracy was 100% using the set threshold.

3.2   Word Error Rate Estimation

Once a document has been identified as one generated by a SR, the next stage will be determining how much error is in the transcript. In speech recognition, the conventional method is to measure the Word Error Rate (WER) by comparing the output of the recogniser to an accurate hand transcription. In the situation we anticipate such a transcript will not be available. In seeking an automatic method for estimating error rates, one should consider how speech recognisers determine the most likely sequence of words that were spoken. In addition to the acoustic models that recognise phonemes, modern SR systems use language models derived from large corpora to determine the most likely word sequence given a set of recognised phonemes. The models are applied over a small sliding window of uttered words (no more than four or five) and have the effect of improving recognition quality.

However, even when incorrectly recognising words, the models produce texts that at the level of word pairs or triples make some form of sense. For example the word sequence "On world news tonight this Wednesday..." is recognised by a poor speech recogniser as "on world is unlike his wins the...": nonsensical, but each word pairing "on world", "world is", "is unlike", "unlike his", "his wins" & "wins the" are sensible when viewed on their own. Consequently, searching a recognised text for unusual word pairs or triples to estimate WER is unlikely to be fruitful. It is better to examine attributes of documents go beyond the local context.

Table 2. Description and WER of SDR 1998 SR systems

Rank	System	Description	WER (%)
1	LTT	Hand transcription of audio data	0.0
2	CU HTK	Cambridge University using HTK toolkit	24.6
3	Dragon	University of Massachusetts & Dragon systems	29.5
4	ATT	AT&T	31.0
5	NIST B1	NIST B1 system	33.8
6	Shef	Sheffield University using Abbot system	35.6
7	NIST B2	NIST B2 system	47.5
8	DERA S2	Defence Evaluation and Research Agency, UK	61.3
9	DERA S1	Defence Evaluation and Research Agency, UK	66.0

The method we propose is based on the observation made in the retrieval experiments of previous work by one of the authors [13]: where ordinary documents were found to be retrieved in preference to the speech recognised. The reason for this was the lower *tf* value of query terms in the recognised documents when compared to the hand transcribed. This was caused by the SR system failing to recognise all occurrences of all the document words and replacing the mis-recognised words with others. We postulate that, in general, the poorer the recognition accuracy of an audio sequence, the greater the number of single occurrence words within the transcription produced. To test this, a small initial experiment was conducted using the TREC SDR 1998 collection: a collection composed of approximately 3,000 short documents transcribed from US news reports. The average number of occurrences of all words in a document was computed and the average of this number was calculated across all documents of the collection. The resulting single value provided a simple measure of how often words are repeated within collection documents. Thanks to efforts by SDR track participants in 1998, transcripts from eight SR runs were made available to fellow participants along with the hand transcription, all shared runs were used in the experiment. As reported by Garofolo et al [16], WERs on the runs varied greatly: the runs plus their error rates are listed in table 2 ranked by WER.

The average term occurrence measure (*to*) for each of the transcripts along with the score for the hand transcript was computed. The results are shown in table 3 with the transcripts ordered by score. As can be seen even in the hand transcription words are rarely used more than once, however the score with one notable exception (i.e. NIST B2) does appear to be ranking systems by their WER.

Table 3. SR systems ranked by term occurrence measure

Rank	System	to	WER Rank
1	LTT	1.28	1
2	CU HTK	1.21	2
3	ATT	1.19	4
4	NIST B1	1.19	5
5	NIST B2	1.18	7
6	Dragon	1.18	3
7	Shef	1.18	6
8	DERA S2	1.13	8
9	DERA S1	1.12	9

Table 4. Systems ranked by modified occurrence measure

Rank	System	to	WER Rank
1	LTT	1.18	1
2	CU HTK	1.12	2
3	NIST B1	1.11	5
4	ATT	1.11	4
5	Dragon	1.10	3
6	Shef	1.09	6
7	NIST B2	1.07	7
8	DERA S2	1.06	8
9	DERA S1	1.05	9

A closer examination of the NIST B2 transcripts indicated that the reason for the high term occurrence measure was due to words with low idf being repeated many times within documents. Consequently the experiment was repeated but with the 1,000 highest frequency words ignored when measuring. The results of this experiment are shown in table 4. (Note, the overall occurrence rate measure is lower for all transcripts, this is to be expected given the removal of the more frequent terms.) Using a simple correlation test, the ranking produced by the altered measure was closer to the WER rate ranking in Garofolo et al's paper.

The result of this experiment was unexpectedly encouraging, however, it must be remembered that the system described so far is only able to rank different recognition outputs of the same transcript. It remains to be seen, if this approach can be extended to compute the accuracy of transcripts from different document sets. In addition, it is also important to recognise that if, as has happened here, a means of automatically measuring the accuracy of a computer program (i.e. the speech recogniser) is devised, then one can use this information to improve the program itself (i.e. improve recogniser accuracy). Therefore, the work of this paper points to the possibility of improving the quality of speech recognisers. Indeed, some initial investigations into SR using a form of *tf* have already taken place [17].

4   Conclusions and Future Work

At the speech retrieval workshop, an alternative approach to achieving fair ranking of different document types was also proposed: here, a mixed collection of speech and hand transcribed documents would, before indexing, be split into separate collections using the spoken document identifier described in Section 3.1. Retrieval would then be conducted on each collection in turn and the ranked list of documents (returned from the two retrievals) merged as occurs in metasearch engines. The means by which the ranks are merged could be based on past retrieval performance or on some merging strategy that locates documents in common to the two collections. Investigating this possible approach will also be a priority of our work.

This paper has described in part, the retrieval problem of the MIND project and described initial work tackling the important challenge of retrieving from collections of documents with varying levels of error within them. A short experiment showed that the proposed ideas are promising and deserving of further investigation and it must be remembered that the method illustrated here only provides a means of ranking transcripts against each other. What is desired is a means of determining levels of error rate from a single transcript. How to achieve this, is our next challenge.

Acknowledgements. This work was funded by the EU 5ᵗʰ Framework project, MIND: IST-2000-26061 (mind.cs.strath.ac.uk).

References

1.   Resource Selection and Data Fusion for Multimedia International Digital Libraries; http://mind.cs.strath.ac.uk/, last accessed: September 2001
2.   John S. Garofolo, Cedric G. P. Auzanne, Ellen M. Voorhees; "The TREC Spoken Document Retrieval Track: A Success Story"; Text Retrieval Conference (TREC) 8, E. Voorhees, Ed.; Gaithersburg, Maryland, USA; November 16-19, 1999
3.   D. Abberley, S. Renals and G. Cook; "Retrieval of broadcast news documents with the THISL system"; In Proceeding *IEEE ICASSP*, pp 3781-3784; Seattle, 1998

4. Steve Renals and Dave Abberley; "The THISL SDR system at TREC-9"; Proceedings of TREC-9; http://www.dcs.shef.ac.uk/~sjr/pubs/2001/trec9.html, last accessed: September 2001

5. The THISL Spoken Document Retrieval Project; http://www.dcs.shef.ac.uk/spandh/projects/thisl/overview-oct98/, last accessed: September 2001

6. Jean-Manuel Van Thong, David Goddeau, Anna Litvinova, Beth Logan, Pedro Moreno and Michael Swain; "SpeechBot: A Speech Recognition based Audio Indexing System for the Web"; *International* Conference on Computer-Assisted Information Retrieval, Recherche d'Informations Assistee par Ordinateur (RIAO2000); Paris, April 2000; pp 106-115

7. Pedro Moreno, JM Van Thong, Beth Logan, Blair Fidler, Katrina Maffey,and Matthew Moores; "SpeechBot: A   Content-based Search Index for Multimedia on the Web"; First IEEE Pacific-Rim Conference on Multimedia, (IEEE-PCM 2000), 2000

8. Compaq Speechbot; http://www.compaq.com/speechbot/, last accessed: September 2001

9. Amit Singhal, Fernando C. N. Pereira; "Document Expansion for Speech Retrieval"; SIGIR 1999; pp34-41

10. M.A. Siegler, M.J. Witbrock, S.T. Slattery, K. Seymore, R.E. Jones and A.G. Hauptmann; "Experiments in Spoken   Document Retrieval at CMU"; Proceeding of the 6th Text REtrieval Conference (TREC 6); November 19-21, 1997; pp291-302

11. G.J.F.Jones and M.Han;   "Retrieving Scanned Documents from a Mixed-Media Document Collection"; Proceedings of the BCS-IRSG European Colloquium on IR Research; Darmstadt, Germany, pp136-149, April 2001

12. Franz J.S. McCarley, S. Roukos; "Ad hoc and Multilingual Information Retrieval at IBM"; Proceeding of The Seventh   Text REtrieval Conference (TREC 7); November 9-11, 1998; pp157-168

13. Mark Sanderson and Fabio Crestani; "Mixing and Merging for Spoken Document Retrieval"; Proceedings of the 2nd European Conference on Digital Libraries; Heraklion, Greece, September 1998, pp397-407. Lecture Notes in Computer Science N. 1513, Springer Verlag, Berlin, Germany.

14. Automatic Language Identification Bibliography; http://speech.inesc.pt/~dcaseiro/html/bibliografia.html, last accessed: September 2001

15. Language   Identification;   http://speech.inesc.pt/~dcaseiro/html/bibliografia.html,   last accessed: September 2001

16. J.S. Garofolo, E.M. Voorhees, C.G.P. Auzanne, M. Stanford, B.A. Lund; "1998 TREC-7 Spoken Document Retrieval Track Overview and Results", in Proceedings of the DARPA Broadcast News Workshop, 1999

17. Yoshihiko Gotoh and Steve Renals; "Variable Word Rate N-Grams"; Proceedings of IEEE ICASSP 2000, pp1591-1594.

The Use of Speech Retrieval Systems: A Study Design

Jinmook Kim and Douglas W. Oard

College of Information Studies and
Institute for Advanced Computer Studies
University of Maryland, College Park, MD 20742-4345, USA
[jinmook, oard]@glue.umd.edu,

Abstract. What criteria for relevance do users apply when selecting a speech recording? What attributes of the recording do they rely on for each criterion? This paper proposes a qualitative research study design to explore those questions. A conceptual framework is presented, research questions are introduced, and the study design is described. The paper concludes with some observations on how the results of the study might inform the design of future systems.

1 Introduction

As the networking and storage infrastructure of the Internet becomes more robust, the potential for physical access to speech recordings is increasing dramatically. Intellectual access is another matter, however, about which less is presently known. We know quite a lot about how people search written text, but the characteristics of recorded speech are sufficiently different that we may ultimately find that users behave differently when searching for speech recordings [4, 9,10,12]. Studying search behavior poses a bit of a chicken-and-egg dilemma, however—we learn what kind of support people need by observing their search behavior, but we cannot observe their behavior until we have built a system that they can search. Internet-based speech retrieval systems are now starting to appear, so we believe this is a propitious time to begin to explore how they are being used. In this paper, we propose the design of a study to examine that question.

2 Conceptual Framework

The concept of relevance is widely used as a basis for evaluating the effectiveness of information retrieval systems [6,8]. Researchers have sought to define relevance from two perspectives that are often referred to as system-oriented and user-oriented. The system-oriented perspective focuses on topical relevance and concerns finding documents that address a concept-based information need. Recall and precision are typically used as measures of effectiveness with this view of

A.R. Coden, E.W. Brown, and S. Srinivasan (Eds.): IR Techniques ..., LNCS 2273, pp. 86–93, 2002.
© Springer-Verlag Berlin Heidelberg 2002

relevance. The user-oriented perspective on relevance is somewhat broader, seeking to characterize the relationship between information and the user's problem situation and attempting to account for the various aspects of human cognitive processes used in making relevance judgments. In this view, common terms that refer to relevance are utility, pertinence, satisfaction, and situational relevance [7, 13]. The user-oriented view does not reject topical relevance—rather it sees it as one of many factors that affect the behavior of searchers [11]. Because we seek to understand search behavior from the broadest possible perspective, we have chosen to adopt a user-oriented view of relevance for our study.

Table 1. Some bases for selecting journal articles.

Criteria	Associated Attributes
Topicality	Title, abstract, keyword
Novelty	Title, abstract, journal name, publication date
Authority	Author, affiliation, journal name, publisher
Recency	Publication date
Reading time	Number of pages
Availability	Owning library
Accessibility	Language, media

The cognitive processes underlying human relevance judgments have been widely studied, often with the goal of identifying factors that influence relevance judgments [1,5,7,11]. Table 1 shows some of the most commonly cited factors that have been identified by previous studies of searchers seeking journal articles. In general, searchers seem to base their assessment of relevance on criteria that they are able to articulate; for example, they may balance the novelty of a document—how new the ideas are to them—with the authority of the source. Criteria such as novelty and authority are abstract concepts, however, so searchers must ground their interpretation of each criterion in some set of document attributes. For example, a searcher might assess the novelty of articles in a journal that they read regularly based solely on the journal name and publication date. For articles in an unfamiliar journal, however, they may need to examine the abstract of each article.

Some of the relevance criteria and attributes identified in Table 1 may be directly applicable to speech recordings, but others may not. Furthermore, the characteristics of specific genres of recorded speech may affect these factors. For example, the distinction between a news program and a news story would be important in news broadcasts, while in recorded classroom lectures the distinctions among course, section (in multi-section courses), and session would be more useful. Table 2 summarizes some relevance criteria and associated attributes that may be applicable to recorded news broadcasts.

Table 2. Possible bases for selecting news broadcasts.

Criteria	Associated Attributes
Topicality	Program title, story title, summary, speaker name
Novelty	Story title, summary, program title, date
Authority	Speaker name, affiliation, program title
Recency	Date
Listening time	Story length
Accessibility	Language, file type

3   Research Design

The goal of our proposed study is to characterize the relevance criteria that searchers apply when searching a collection of recorded radio programs and the attributes of the recordings on which those criteria are based. We seek to focus on understanding how users perceive relevance; at this stage, we are interested in the cognitive process that results in a relevance judgment, not just in the outcome of the judgment process. Qualitative research methods are well suited to a study of this type [2,3], so we have adopted a research design based on case studies, one of the most widely used qualitative methods.

3.1   Research Questions

The central issue that we wish to understand is how searchers decide which recordings are relevant to their needs when using an interactive retrieval system. In order to explore this issue, we have adopted the following "foreshadowing questions" to focus our inquiry:

a. What criteria do searchers rely on when choosing a recording?
b. How do searchers integrate multiple criteria when deciding whether to select a document?
c. What attributes of the recordings do searchers use as a basis for assessing each relevance criterion?
d. How do searchers integrate evidence from multiple attributes when assessing the relevance of a document?
e. What presentation strategies best convey useful attribute information to searchers?

3.2   Search Systems

Two broad classes of audio search technology have emerged on the Web. National Public Radio's NPR Online (http://www.npr.org/archives) is an example of a site that supports searching based on manually prepared transcripts, summaries, and/or metadata. Compaq's SpeechBot (http://speechbot.com) is an example of an alternative approach in which speech recognition technology is used in conjunction with a limited amount of automatically obtained metadata such as date and source to support searches. Fortuitously, NPR Online and SpeechBot index some of the same programs, including American RadioWorks, Car Talk, The Diane Rehm Show, Fresh Air, Marketplace, and Public Interest. Each system accepts a text query, optionally with some desired values for metadata (e.g., date), and returns a list of hits in order of decreasing likelihood that the recording will satisfy the query based on the information that is indexed. The systems differ in terms of what is indexed, the information displayed for the search results, and other user interface design details. Each system allows searchers to replay part or all of each program that is presented in the search results (in each case, using RealPlayer). We plan to use both NPR online and SpeechBot in order to explore a broader range of issues than would be possible with either system alone.

3.3   Participants

Ideally, we would like to explore the behavior of experienced searchers using a system with which they are familiar. Web-based audio searching is still relatively new, however, so it would be difficult to identify participants for our study that have these characteristics. We have therefore chosen to recruit from an accessible group of potential participants that approximates these desirable characteristics to some degree. Our participants will be students enrolled in a Fall 2001 graduate-level seminar on visual and sound materials, in which students study acquisition, preservation, access, and management issues. All the students have completed a prerequisite course on information access, but few have prior experience with audio searching.

4   Data Collection

The goal of our data collection plan is to provide insight into the cognitive processes underlying human relevance judgments for recorded speech. Our focus is not on the results of the process, but rather on the process itself: the relevance criteria that our participants apply and the attributes of the recordings on which those criteria are based. To gain insight into that process, we will use observation and think-aloud during each search and one semi-structured interview at the end of the session. Each participant will be asked to perform a series of searches. The first two searches will be conducted using a single system and two topics chosen by the investigators: one narrow question that could be answered using the content of a single recording, and one broader topic. Some participants will search recordings using NPR Online for both topics, the others will use SpeechBot. Each participant will then be asked to perform third search based on his or her own information needs using the same system. They then will be offered the opportunity to search for additional stories that satisfy their personal information needs using the other system. This study design will permit some degree of cross-system comparison while limiting the length of each session.

During each search, an observer will make notes that capture the observer's impression of the searcher's behavior using our criteria/attribute framework. While searching, each participant will also be asked to think aloud, explaining in his/her own words why he/she selected a specific recording using what attributes or took some other action. Finally, a semi-structured interview will be conducted at the end of the session to obtain additional insight into the relevance criteria and attributes that each participant used to find relevant recordings. We expect that a typical session will take less than two hours, but each participant will be allowed to continue his or her search as long as desired. The anonymity of participants will be protected by coding all records with a participant number rather than a name and by limiting access to information that might tend to reveal the identity of an individual participant.

4.1   Observational Protocol

The focus of the observer's activity will be on understanding how the searcher chooses to select or not to select a recording, not on how well the results actually meet their needs. Any unexpected behavior may also be noted and used to guide clarification questions during the interview. The observer will not interrupt the searcher during a search, and searchers will be asked not to consult the observer as a source of expert advice during the session. The observer may, however, help the user start the Web browser and reach the appropriate search page, since those are not tasks that we seek to study.

4.2   Think-Aloud Protocol

Think-aloud methods have both advantages and disadvantages as a component of qualitative study designs. One important concern is that verbalizing thoughts can inspire introspection, which in turn might alter the behavior that we wish to study. On the positive side, however, think-aloud can provide insights into the cognitive processes of a searcher that may not be available in any other way. We have considered these factors and chosen to ask participants to think aloud. Some brief training on the think-aloud process will be given immediately before the actual session. We will inform the participants of our interest in the way they select recordings, but we do not plan to provide them with specific guidelines on what we want them to talk about or how they should express their thoughts. With the consent of each participant, the think-aloud will be audiotaped and subsequently transcribed.

4.3   Interview Protocol

A semi-structured interview will be conducted immediately following each participant's last search. The goal of the interview is to obtain additional information about the process by which a participant made relevance judgments. With the consent of the participant, the interviews will be audiotaped and subsequently transcribed. The topics that will be explored and a suggested question that can be used to initiate discussion on each topic are:

1. What relevance criteria were applied in some specific cases? (Suggested question: Why did you choose to listen to [some specific recording]?)
2. In those cases, how were the criteria used together to reach a decision? (Suggested question: Were some factors more important than others?)
3. In those cases, how were attributes of the recordings used as a basis for assessing each relevance criterion? (Suggested question: How did you determine that the [topic was appropriate, source was authoritative, etc.])
4. What aspects of the design of each system were beneficial? (Suggested question: What features of each system were most helpful?)
5. What capabilities were not present in either system that would have been desirable? (Suggested question: Were there any features that you had expected to see in an audio search system that were not present in either system?)

5 Data Analysis

Observational notes, think-aloud transcripts, and semi-structured interview transcripts will be categorized based on a conceptual framework evolved from the relevance criteria and attributes identified in Table 2. New categories will be created if the analysis reveals additional criteria and/or attributes. The QSR NUD*IST system provides extensive support for qualitative analysis of coded datasets, so we plan to code our categories for use with that software. We will seek to confirm indications obtained from one data source using another, a process known as triangulation, in order to gain confidence in the reliability of our interpretations. As we learn more about the cognitive processes of early participants, we will use that understanding to guide our design of probing questions in subsequent semi-structured interviews with other participants. We plan to employ matrices resembling Table 2 that will explore patterns and trends in the application of relevance criteria and associated attributes to make decisions.

6 Validity Issues

Our study design includes purposive sampling of the possible searcher population, but the limited experience of our participants does pose a threat to the validity of our study that we will need to recognize when reporting our findings. We will take three steps to enhance the validity of our analysis: triangulation (described above), member checks, and peer debriefing. The participants in our study (the "members") are certainly in the best position to assess whether we have interpreted their actions and statements correctly, so we plan to check our results with them in two ways. First, we plan to meet privately with some of our participants to discuss our findings and the manner in which we reached those conclusions. Second, we will offer to present our research results to the class near the end of the semester and solicit their comments.

Qualitative study designs rely heavily on subjective interpretation, so the validity of the analytic process is also an important concern. Member checks offer excellent insight into the validity of our interpretations, but they cannot ensure that our analysis process is applied in an appropriate way. For this reason, we will ask some of our colleagues at the University of Maryland with experience in qualitative research to review our categorization, coding and analysis processes.

7 Conclusion

Speech retrieval systems are now beginning to appear on the Internet, but it is not yet clear how these systems will be used. We believe that the question of how people will use such systems is best explored using qualitative research methods, and in this paper we have proposed the design of a case study. Although our usage scenario is necessarily somewhat artificial, we believe that our proposed study can offer a useful degree of insight into the issues that we have raised. It is our hope that the insights that we gain will be of benefit to the designers of future speech retrieval systems. With that in mind, we feel that it is important to help advance the dialog between those who build systems and those who study their use. Perhaps our discussion of this study design can be one step in that direction.

Acknowledgments. The authors are grateful to Delia Neuman, the reviewers, and the workshop participants for thoughtful comments on earlier drafts of this paper, Thomas Connors for inviting us to work with his class, and Compaq Corporate Research and National Public Radio for making their systems available.

References

1. C.L. Barry. User-defined relevance criteria: An exploratory study. *Journal of the American Society for Information Science*, 45(3):149–159, 1994.
2. J.W. Creswell. *Research Deisgn: Qualitative and Quantitative Approaches.* Sage Publications Inc., Thousand Oaks: CA, 1994.
3. J.A. Maxwell. *Qualitative Research Design: An Interactive Approach.* Sage Publications, Inc., Thousand Oaks: CA, 1996.
4. Douglas W. Oard. User interface design for speech-based retrieval. *Bulletin of the American Society for Information Science*, 25(5):20–22, 2000.
5. T.K. Park. The nature of relevance in information retrieval: An empirical study. *Library Quarterly*, 63(3):318–351, 1993.
6. T. Saracevic. Relevance: A review of a framework for the thinking on the notion in information science. *Advances in Librarianship*, 6:79–138, 1976.
7. L. Schamber. Revance and information behavior. *Annual Review of Information Science and Technology*, 29:1–48, 1994.
8. L. Schamber, M.B. Eisenberg, and M.S. Nilan. A re-examination of relevance: Toward a dynamic, situational definition. *Information Processing and Management*, 26(6):755–766, 1990.
9. L. Slaughter, D.W. Oard, V.L. Warnick, J.L. Harding, and G.J. Wilkerson. A graphical interface for speech-based retrieval. In *The Third ACM Conference on Digital Libraries*, 1998.

10. T. Tombros and F. Crestani. Users' perception of relevance of spoken documents. *JASIS*, 51(10):929–939, 2000.

11. P. Wang and D. Soergel. A cognitive model of document use during a research project. *Journal of the American Society for Information Science*, 49(2):115–133, 1998.

12. S. Whittaker, J. Hirschberg, and C.H. Nakatani. Play it again: A study of the factors underlying speech browsing behavior. In *Proceedings of ACM CHI 98*, pages 18–23, April 1998.

13. P. Wilson. Situational relevance. *Information Storage and Retrieval*, 9:457–471, 1973.

Speech-Driven Text Retrieval: Using Target IR Collections for Statistical Language Model Adaptation in Speech Recognition

Atsushi Fujii[1], Katunobu Itou[2], and Tetsuya Ishikawa[1]

[1] University of Library and Information Science
1-2 Kasuga, Tsukuba, 305-8550, Japan
{fujii,ishikawa}@ulis.ac.jp
[2] National Institute of Advanced Industrial Science and Technology
1-1-1 Chuuou Daini Umezono, Tsukuba, 305-8568, Japan
itou@ni.aist.go.jp

Abstract. Speech recognition has of late become a practical technology for real world applications. Aiming at speech-driven text retrieval, which facilitates retrieving information with spoken queries, we propose a method to integrate speech recognition and retrieval methods. Since users speak contents related to a target collection, we adapt statistical language models used for speech recognition based on the target collection, so as to improve both the recognition and retrieval accuracy. Experiments using existing test collections combined with dictated queries showed the effectiveness of our method.

1 Introduction

Automatic speech recognition, which decodes human voice to generate transcriptions, has of late become a practical technology. It is feasible that speech recognition is used in real world computer-based applications, specifically, those associated with human language. In fact, a number of speech-based methods have been explored in the information retrieval community, which can be classified into the following two fundamental categories:

- spoken document retrieval, in which written queries are used to search speech (e.g., broadcast news audio) archives for relevant speech information [5,6,15, 16,17,19,20],
- speech-driven (spoken query) retrieval, in which spoken queries are used to retrieve relevant textual information [2,3].

Initiated partially by the TREC-6 spoken document retrieval (SDR) track [4], various methods have been proposed for spoken document retrieval. However, a relatively small number of methods have been explored for speech-driven text retrieval, although they are associated with numerous keyboard-less retrieval applications, such as telephone-based retrieval, car navigation systems, and user-friendly interfaces.

A.R. Coden, E.W. Brown, and S. Srinivasan (Eds.): IR Techniques ..., LNCS 2273, pp. 94–104, 2002.

Barnett et al. [2] performed comparative experiments related to speech-driven retrieval, where an existing speech recognition system was used as an input interface for the INQUERY text retrieval system. They used as test inputs 35 queries collected from the TREC 101-135 topics, dictated by a single male speaker. Crestani [3] also used the above 35 queries and showed that conventional relevance feedback techniques marginally improved the accuracy for speech-driven text retrieval.

These above cases focused solely on improving text retrieval methods and did not address problems of improving speech recognition accuracy. In fact, an existing speech recognition system was used with no enhancement. In other words, speech recognition and text retrieval modules were fundamentally independent and were simply connected by way of an input/output protocol.

However, since most speech recognition systems are trained based on specific domains, the accuracy of speech recognition across domains is not satisfactory. Thus, as can easily be predicted, in cases of Barnett et al. [2] and Crestani [3], a relatively high speech recognition error rate considerably decreased the retrieval accuracy. Additionally, speech recognition with a high accuracy is crucial for interactive retrieval.

Motivated by these problems, in this paper we integrate (not simply connect) speech recognition and text retrieval to improve both recognition and retrieval accuracy in the context of speech-driven text retrieval.

Unlike general-purpose speech recognition aimed to decode any spontaneous speech, in the case of speech-driven text retrieval, users usually speak contents associated with a target collection, from which documents relevant to their information need are retrieved. In a stochastic speech recognition framework, the accuracy depends primarily on acoustic and language models [1]. While acoustic models are related to phonetic properties, language models, which represent linguistic contents to be spoken, are strongly related to target collections. Thus, it is intuitively feasible that language models have to be produced based on target collections.

To sum up, our belief is that by adapting a language model based on a target IR collection, we can improve the speech recognition and text retrieval accuracy, simultaneously.

Section 2 describes our prototype speech-driven text retrieval system, which is currently implemented for Japanese. Section 3 elaborates on comparative experiments, in which existing test collections for Japanese text retrieval are used to evaluate the effectiveness of our system.

2 System Description

2.1 Overview

Figure 1 depicts the overall design of our speech-driven text retrieval system, which consists of speech recognition, text retrieval and adaptation modules. We explain the retrieval process based on this figure.

In the off-line process, the adaptation module uses the entire target collection (from which relevant documents are retrieved) to produce a language model, so that user speech related to the collection can be recognized with a high accuracy. On the other hand, an acoustic model is produced independent of the target collection.

In the on-line process, given an information need spoken by a user, the speech recognition module uses the acoustic and language models to generate a transcription for the user speech. Then, the text retrieval module searches the collection for documents relevant to the transcription, and outputs a specific number of top-ranked documents according to the degree of relevance, in descending order.

These documents are fundamentally final outputs. However, in the case where the target collection consists of multiple domains, a language model produced in the off-line adaptation process is not necessarily precisely adapted to a specific information need. Thus, we optionally use top-ranked documents obtained in the initial retrieval process for an on-line adaptation, because these documents are associated with the user speech more than the entire collection. We then re-perform speech recognition and text retrieval processes to obtain final outputs.

In other words, our system is based on the two-stage retrieval principle [8], where top-ranked documents retrieved in the first stage are intermediate results, and are used to improve the accuracy for the second (final) stage. From a different perspective, while the off-line adaptation process produces the *global* language model for a target collection, the on-line adaptation process produces a *local* language model based on the user speech.

In the following sections, we explain speech recognition, adaptation, and text retrieval modules in Figure 1, respectively.

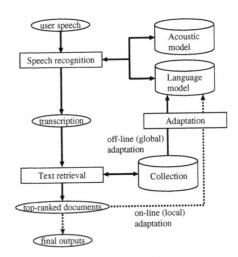

Fig. 1. The overall design of our speech-driven text retrieval system.

2.2   Speech Recognition

The speech recognition module generates word sequence W, given phoneme sequence X. In the stochastic speech recognition framework, the task is to output the W maximizing $P(W|X)$, which is transformed as in equation (1) through use of the Bayesian theorem.

$$\arg\max_{W} P(W|X) = \arg\max_{W} P(X|W) \cdot P(W) \tag{1}$$

Here, $P(X|W)$ models a probability that word sequence W is transformed into phoneme sequence X, and $P(W)$ models a probability that W is linguistically acceptable. These factors are usually called acoustic and language models, respectively.

For the speech recognition module, we use the Japanese dictation toolkit [7][1], which includes the "Julius" recognition engine and acoustic/language models trained based on newspaper articles. This toolkit also includes development software, so that acoustic and language models can be produced and replaced depending on the application. While we use the acoustic model provided in the toolkit, we use new language models produced by way of the adaptation process (see Section 2.3).

2.3   Language Model Adaptation

The basis of the adaptation module is to produce a word-based N-gram (in our case, a combination of bigram and trigram) model by way of source documents.

In the off-line (global) adaptation process, we use the ChaSen morphological analyzer [10] to extract words from the entire target collection, and produce the global N-gram model.

On the other hand, in the on-line (local) adaptation process, only top-ranked documents retrieved in the first stage are used as source documents, from which word-based N-grams are extracted as performed in the off-line process. However, unlike the case of the off-line process, we do not produce the entire language model. Instead, we re-estimate only statistics associated with top-ranked documents, for which we use the MAP (Maximum A-posteriori Probability) estimation method [9].

Although the on-line adaptation theoretically improves the retrieval accuracy, for real-time usage, the trade-off between the retrieval accuracy and computational time required for the on-line process has to be considered.

Our method is similar to the one proposed by Seymore and Rosenfeld [14] in the sense that both methods adapt language models based on a small number of documents related to a specific domain (or topic). However, unlike their method, our method does not require corpora manually annotated with topic tags.

---

[1] http://winnie.kuis.kyoto-u.ac.jp/dictation/

2.4   Text Retrieval

The text retrieval module is based on an existing probabilistic retrieval method described in [13], which computes the relevance score between the transcribed query and each document in the collection. The relevance score for document i is computed based on equation (2).

$$\sum_t \left(\frac{TF_{t,i}}{\frac{DL_i}{avglen} + TF_{t,i}} \cdot \log \frac{N}{DF_t} \right) \tag{2}$$

Here, t's denote terms in transcribed queries. $TF_{t,i}$ denotes the frequency that term t appears in document i. DF_t and N denote the number of documents containing term t and the total number of documents in the collection. DL_i denotes the length of document i (i.e., the number of characters contained in i), and $avglen$ denotes the average length of documents in the collection.

We use content words extracted from documents as terms, and perform a word-based indexing. For this purpose, we use the ChaSen morphological analyzer [10] to extract content words. We extract terms from transcribed queries using the same method.

3   Experimentation

3.1   Test Collections

We investigated the performance of our system based on the NTCIR workshop evaluation methodology, which resembles the one in the TREC ad hoc retrieval track. In other words, each system outputs 1,000 top documents, and the TREC evaluation software was used to plot recall-precision curves and calculate non-interpolated average precision values.

The NTCIR workshop was held twice (in 1999 and 2001), for which two different test collections were produced: the NTCIR-1 and 2 collections [11,12][2]. However, since these collections do not include spoken queries, we asked four speakers (two males/females) to dictate information needs in the NTCIR collections, and simulated speech-driven text retrieval.

The NTCIR collections include documents collected from technical papers published by 65 Japanese associations for various fields. Each document consists of the document ID, title, name(s) of author(s), name/date of conference, hosting organization, abstract and author keywords, from which we used titles, abstracts and keywords for the indexing. The number of documents in the NTCIR-1 and 2 collections are 332,918 and 736,166, respectively (the NTCIR-1 documents are a subset of the NTCIR-2).

The NTCIR-1 and 2 collections also include 53 and 49 topics, respectively. Each topic consists of the topic ID, title of the topic, description, narrative.

---

[2] http://research.nii.ac.jp/~ntcadm/index-en.html

Figure 2 shows an English translation for a fragment of the NTCIR topics[3], where each field is tagged in an SGML form. In general, titles are not informative for the retrieval. On the other hand, narratives, which usually consist of several sentences, are too long to speak. Thus, only descriptions, which consist of a single phrase and sentence, were dictated by each speaker, so as to produce four different sets of 102 spoken queries.

```
<TOPIC q=0118>
<TITLE>TV conferencing</TITLE>
<DESCRIPTION>Distance education support systems using TV
conferencing</DESCRIPTION>
<NARRATIVE>A relevant document will provide information on
the development of distance education support systems using TV
conferencing. Preferred documents would present examples of using
TV conferencing and discuss the results. Any reported methods
of aiding remote teaching are relevant documents (for example,
ways of utilizing satellite communication, the Internet, and ISDN
circuits).</NARRATIVE>
</TOPIC>
```

Fig. 2. An English translation for an example topic in the NTCIR collections.

In the NTCIR collections, relevance assessment was performed based on the pooling method [18]. First, candidates for relevant documents were obtained with multiple retrieval systems. Then, for each candidate document, human expert(s) assigned one of three ranks of relevance: "relevant," "partially relevant" and "irrelevant." The NTCIR-2 collection also includes "highly relevant" documents. In our evaluation, "highly relevant" and "relevant" documents were regarded as relevant ones.

3.2 Comparative Evaluation

In order to investigate the effectiveness of the off-line language model adaptation, we compared the performance of the following different retrieval methods:

- text-to-text retrieval, which used written descriptions as queries, and can be seen as the perfect speech-driven text retrieval,
- speech-driven text retrieval, in which a language model produced based on the NTCIR-2 collection was used,
- speech-driven text retrieval, in which a language model produced based on ten years worth of *Mainichi Shimbun* Japanese newspaper articles (1991-2000) was used.

---

[3] The NTCIR-2 collection contains Japanese topics and their English translations.

The only difference in producing two different language models (i.e., those based on the NTCIR-2 collection and newspaper articles) are the source documents. In other words, both language models have the same vocabulary size (20,000), and were produced using the same software.

Table 1 shows statistics related to word tokens/types in two different source corpora for language modeling, where the line "Coverage" denotes the ratio of word tokens contained in the resultant language model. Most of word tokens were covered in both language models.

Table 1. Statistics associated with source words for language modeling.

	NTCIR	News
# of Types	454K	315K
# of Tokens	175M	262M
Coverage	97.9%	96.5%

In cases of speech-driven text retrieval methods, queries dictated by four speakers were used individually. Thus, in practice we compared nine different retrieval methods. Although the Julius decoder outputs more than one transcription candidate for a single speech input, we used only the one with the greatest probability score. The results did not significantly change depending on whether or not we used lower-ranked transcriptions as queries.

Table 2 shows the non-interpolated average precision values and word error rate in speech recognition, for different retrieval methods. As with existing experiments for speech recognition, word error rate (WER) is the ratio between the number of word errors (i.e., deletion, insertion, and substitution) and the total number of words. In addition, we also investigated error rate with respect to query terms (i.e., keywords used for retrieval), which we shall call "term error rate (TER)."

In Table 2, the first line denotes results of the text-to-text retrieval, which were relatively high compared with existing results reported in the NTCIR workshops [11,12].

The remaining lines denote results of speech-driven text retrieval combined with the NTCIR-based language model (lines 2-5) and the newspaper-based model (lines 6-9), respectively. Here, "Mx" and "Fx" denote male/female speakers, respectively. Suggestions which can be derived from these results are as follows.

First, for both language models, results did not significantly change depending on the speaker. The best average precision values for speech-driven text retrieval were obtained with a combination of queries dictated by a male speaker (M1) and the NTCIR-based language model, which were approximately 80% of those with the text-to-text retrieval.

Table 2. Results for different retrieval methods (AP: average precision, WER: word error rate, TER: term error rate).

Method	NTCIR-1			NTCIR-2		
	AP	WER	TER	AP	WER	TER
Text	0.3320	—	—	0.3118	—	—
M1 (NTCIR)	0.2708	0.1659	0.2190	0.2504	0.1532	0.2313
M2 (NTCIR)	0.2471	0.2034	0.2381	0.2114	0.2180	0.2799
F1 (NTCIR)	0.2276	0.1961	0.2857	0.1873	0.1885	0.2500
F2 (NTCIR)	0.2642	0.1477	0.2222	0.2376	0.1635	0.2388
M1 (News)	0.1076	0.3547	0.5143	0.0790	0.3594	0.5149
M2 (News)	0.1257	0.4044	0.5460	0.0691	0.5022	0.6343
F1 (News)	0.1156	0.3801	0.5238	0.0798	0.4418	0.5709
F2 (News)	0.1225	0.3317	0.5016	0.0917	0.4080	0.5858

Second, by comparing results of different language models for each speaker, one can see that the NTCIR-based model significantly decreased WER and TER obtained with the newspaper-based model, and that the retrieval method using the NTCIR-based model significantly outperformed one using the newspaper-based model. Furthermore, these results were observable irrespective of the speaker. Thus, we conclude that adapting language models based on target collections was quite effective for speech-driven text retrieval.

Third, TER was generally higher than WER irrespective of the speaker. In other words, speech recognition for content words was more difficult than functional words, which were not contained in query terms.

We analyzed transcriptions for dictated queries, and found that speech recognition error was mainly caused by the out-of-vocabulary problem. In the case where major query terms are mistakenly recognized, the retrieval accuracy substantially decreases. In addition, descriptions in the NTCIR topics often contain expressions which do not appear in the documents, such as "I want papers about..." Although these expressions usually do not affect the retrieval accuracy, misrecognized words affect the recognition accuracy for remaining words including major query terms. Consequently, the retrieval accuracy decreases due to the partial misrecognition.

Finally, we investigated the trade-off between recall and precision. Figures 3 and 4 show recall-precision curves of different retrieval methods, for the NTCIR-1 and 2 collections, respectively. In these figures, the relative superiority for precision values due to different language models in Table 2 was also observable, regardless of the recall.

However, the effectiveness of the on-line adaptation remains an open question and needs to be explored.

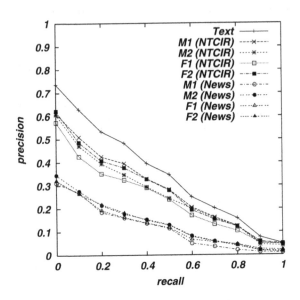

Fig. 3. Recall-precision curves for different retrieval methods using the NTCIR-1 collection.

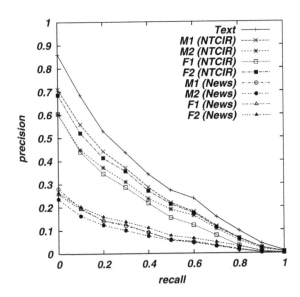

Fig. 4. Recall-precision curves for different retrieval methods using the NTCIR-2 collection.

4   Conclusion

Aiming at speech-driven text retrieval with a high accuracy, we proposed a method to integrate speech recognition and text retrieval methods, in which target text collections are used to adapt statistical language models for speech recognition. We also showed the effectiveness of our method by way of experiments, where dictated information needs in the NTCIR collections were used as queries to retrieve technical abstracts. Future work would include experiments on various collections, such as newspaper articles and Web pages.

Acknowledgments. The authors would like to thank the National Institute of Informatics for their support with the NTCIR collections.

References

1. L. R. Bahl, F. Jelinek, and R. L. Mercer. A maximum likelihood approach to continuous speech recognition. *IEEE Transactions on Pattern Analysis and Machine Intelligence*, 5(2):179–190, 1983.
2. J. Barnett, S. Anderson, J. Broglio, M. Singh, R. Hudson, and S. W. Kuo. Experiments in spoken queries for document retrieval. In *Proceedings of Eurospeech97*, pages 1323–1326, 1997.
3. F. Crestani. Word recognition errors and relevance feedback in spoken query processing. In *Proceedings of the Fourth International Conference on Flexible Query Answering Systems*, pages 267–281, 2000.
4. J. S. Garofolo, E. M. Voorhees, V. M. Stanford, and K. S. Jones. TREC-6 1997 spoken document retrieval track overview and results. In *Proceedings of the 6th Text REtrieval Conference*, pages 83–91, 1997.
5. S. Johnson, P. Jourlin, G. Moore, K. S. Jones, and P. Woodland. The Cambridge University spoken document retrieval system. In *Proceedings of ICASSP'99*, pages 49–52, 1999.
6. G. Jones, J. Foote, K. S. Jones, and S. Young. Retrieving spoken documents by combining multiple index sources. In *Proceedings of the 19th Annual International ACM SIGIR Conference on Research and Development in Information Retrieval*, pages 30–38, 1996.
7. T. Kawahara, A. Lee, T. Kobayashi, K. Takeda, N. Minematsu, S. Sagayama, K. Itou, A. Ito, M. Yamamoto, A. Yamada, T. Utsuro, and K. Shikano. Free software toolkit for Japanese large vocabulary continuous speech recognition. In *Proceedings of the 6th International Conference on Spoken Language Processing*, pages 476–479, 2000.
8. K. Kwok and M. Chan. Improving two-stage ad-hoc retrieval for short queries. In *Proceedings of the 21st Annual International ACM SIGIR Conference on Research and Development in Information Retrieval*, pages 250–256, 1998.
9. H. Masataki, Y. Sagisaka, K. Hisaki, and T. Kawahara. Task adaptation using MAP estimation in n-gram language modeling. In *Proceedings of ICASSP'97*, pages 783–786, 1997.
10. Y. Matsumoto, A. Kitauchi, T. Yamashita, Y. Hirano, H. Matsuda, and M. Asahara. Japanese morphological analysis system ChaSen version 2.0 manual 2nd edition. Technical Report NAIST-IS-TR99009, NAIST, 1999.

11. National Center for Science Information Systems. *Proceedings of the 1st NTCIR Workshop on Research in Japanese Text Retrieval and Term Recognition*, 1999.
12. National Institute of Informatics. *Proceedings of the 2nd NTCIR Workshop Meeting on Evaluation of Chinese & Japanese Text Retrieval and Text Summarization*, 2001.
13. S. Robertson and S. Walker. Some simple effective approximations to the 2-poisson model for probabilistic weighted retrieval. In *Proceedings of the 17th Annual International ACM SIGIR Conference on Research and Development in Information Retrieval*, pages 232–241, 1994.
14. K. Seymore and R. Rosenfeld. Using story topics for language model adaptation. In *Proceedings of Eurospeech97*, 1997.
15. P. Sheridan, M. Wechsler, and P. Schäuble. Cross-language speech retrieval: Establishing a baseline performance. In *Proceedings of the 20th Annual International ACM SIGIR Conference on Research and Development in Information Retrieval*, pages 99–108, 1997.
16. A. Singhal and F. Pereira. Document expansion for speech retrieval. In *Proceedings of the 22nd Annual International ACM SIGIR Conference on Research and Development in Information Retrieval*, pages 34–41, 1999.
17. S. Srinivasan and D. Petkovic. Phonetic confusion matrix based spoken document retrieval. In *Proceedings of the 23rd Annual International ACM SIGIR Conference on Research and Development in Information Retrieval*, pages 81–87, 2000.
18. E. M. Voorhees. Variations in relevance judgments and the measurement of retrieval effectiveness. In *Proceedings of the 21st Annual International ACM SIGIR Conference on Research and Development in Information Retrieval*, pages 315–323, 1998.
19. M. Wechsler, E. Munteanu, and P. Schäuble. New techniques for open-vocabulary spoken document retrieval. In *Proceedings of the 21st Annual International ACM SIGIR Conference on Research and Development in Information Retrieval*, pages 20–27, 1998.
20. S. Whittaker, J. Hirschberg, J. Choi, D. Hindle, F. Pereira, and A. Singhal. SCAN: Designing and evaluating user interfaces to support retrieval from speech archives. In *Proceedings of the 22nd Annual International ACM SIGIR Conference on Research and Development in Information Retrieval*, pages 26–33, 1999.

WASABI: Framework for Real-Time Speech Analysis Applications (Demo)*

Eric W. Brown and Anni R. Coden

IBM T.J. Watson Research Center, Yorktown Heights, NY 10598
ewb@us.ibm.com, anni@us.ibm.com

Abstract. Speech is a tantalizing mode of human communication. On the one hand, humans understand speech with ease and use speech to express complex ideas, information, and knowledge. On the other hand, automatic speech recognition with computers is still very hard, and extracting knowledge from speech is even harder. We have developed a framework for analyzing speech that enables the incorporation of speech into a variety of information and knowledge management applications. We briefly describe the framework and demonstrate two applications that use the framework.

1 Introduction

Spoken discourse includes any spoken conversation between two or more individuals that takes place anywhere, any time. Spoken discourse is a rich source of tacit information, and often the only form in which the tacit information is instantiated. Until very recently, it was nearly impossible to capture and exploit this information. Recent advances in speech recognition technology, however, have enabled the exploration and development of a number of interesting technologies and applications that attempt to capture spoken discourse, convert the discourse to text, apply text analysis to the discourse, and exploit the knowledge discovered in the discourse.

A recent research focus at the IBM T.J. Watson Research Center has been the problem of how to capture spoken discourse and analyze it in real-time to both extract knowledge from the discourse and provide additional, related knowledge to the discourse participants. The need for this capability is driven by two separate applications: meeting support and data broadcasting. Meeting support in this context includes the ability to understand the current meeting discussion and automatically provide related information to the meeting participants. Data broadcasting is the process of exploiting the unused bandwidth in a television broadcast to send arbitrary data with the television program. In particular, the data should be related to the current television program and enable an enhanced viewing experience for the user where the audio/visual television program is enriched with related facts, articles, and references.

---

* Abstracted, with permission, from "Towards Speech as a Knowledge Resource," IBM Systems Journal 40, No. 4, (2001)

A.R. Coden, E.W. Brown, and S. Srinivasan (Eds.): IR Techniques ..., LNCS 2273, pp. 105–108, 2002.
© Springer-Verlag Berlin Heidelberg 2002

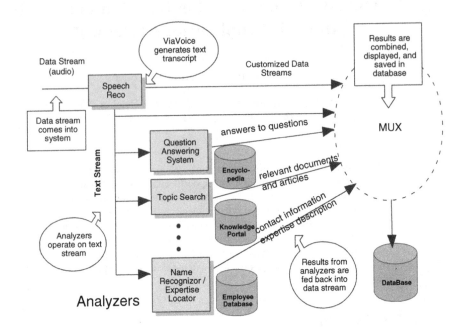

Fig. 1. WASABI architecture

2   WASABI

To explore these problems we have developed the WASABI framework for analyzing speech, (Watson Automatic Stream Analysis for Broadcast Information)[2]. WASABI takes speech audio as input, converts the audio stream into text using a speech recognition system, applies a variety of analyzers to the text stream to identify information elements, automatically generates queries from these information elements, and extracts data from the search results that is relevant to the current discourse. Figure 1 shows the overall architecture.

The input to the system is the raw data stream, i.e., the captured audio of the discourse. The speech recognition system, IBM ViaVoice™, converts the audio into a text stream, which WASABI feeds to one or more *analyzers*. An analyzer performs a text analysis procedure on its input and produces an output that may be fed to another analyzer or multiplexed back into the original data stream. The task performed by each analyzer depends on the application in which the framework is applied. One of the more important tasks performed by an analyzer is to automatically create a query from the input, use the query to search a relevant knowledge repository, and extract relevant information from the search results that will enhance the input data stream.

2.1   MeetingMiner

The first application area addressed by the WASABI framework is meetings, which are an obvious source of knowledge in any organization. They occur regularly and in a variety of settings, and often suffer from two problems. First, depending on the formality of the meeting, the content of the meeting will be captured with limited success. More formal meetings may have actual minutes created by a designated scribe, while less formal meetings will be captured only by the notes taken by the meeting participants, or worse, the collective memory of the participants. The second problem common to most meetings is that during the meeting the participants do not have convenient access to all of the knowledge resources that might be used to facilitate or enrich the meeting. These resources might be as simple as someone's phone number, or they might be more complex, such as a project database that identifies who is working on what and where expertise on a particular topic can be found.

The WASABI framework is being applied to solve these problems in a system called MeetingMiner. The system is essentially an agent that passively captures and analyzes the meeting discussion, and periodically becomes an active participant in the meeting whenever it finds information that it determines is highly pertinent to the current discussion. The main input to the system is an audio stream generated by one or more microphones that capture the spoken discourse of the meeting. The audio stream is converted to a text transcript by the speech recognition system, and the text transcript is processed by the meeting analyzers, which include a named entity recognizer, a topic tracker, and a question identifier tied to a question answering system [3]. The system presents relevant collateral information found by the analyzers using a graphical display or speech synthesis.

2.2   Data Broadcast

The second use of the WASABI framework is to support *data broadcasting*, which is the process of transmitting arbitrary data in the unused bandwidth of a television broadcast[2]. A high definition television (HDTV) channel has over 1.5 Mbits/sec of bandwidth available to send data in addition to the audio and video program. This bandwidth can be used to send any data that the receiver is capable of processing, though one appealing use of the bandwidth is to send collateral information related to the currently broadcast television program. For example, if the current broadcast is a news program, the data channel might contain text versions of related stories, biographies of people mentioned in the news, geographical information for places mentioned, or links (URLs) to World Wide Web pages that contain additional information. This is clearly useful in a knowledge management context where information (e.g., news, training, reports, etc.) is distributed in the form of video programs. The WASABI analysis can automatically enrich the video with related facts and data from knowledge repositories of particular interest to the end user.

The overall processing flow for data broadcasting is very similar to that used in the MeetingMiner system. The audio/video source is fed to a collection of real time feature extractors that extract text and possibly other visual features. In particular, the system uses speech recognition to generate a text transcript. The analyzers classify the text into topics, extract named entities (e.g., names of people, places, dates, etc.), and automatically generate queries to retrieve relevant information from related databases.

3   Conclusions

Successful knowledge management applications will ultimately need to solve the problem of capturing and exploiting tacit knowledge. Current solutions that focus on structured data and semi-structured documents are limited to the knowledge that users are willing (or forced) to enter in these forms. Even when users wish to document their knowledge, they may be unable to articulate the tacit knowledge that they use daily in an almost subconscious manner. This leaves us with only the words and actions of the user as an explicit representation of the tacit knowledge they posses. Fortunately, we can easily capture words and actions with audio and video recordings. The challenge is processing these recordings and extracting the knowledge in a form amenable to further analysis and reuse.

We are exploring a number of applications that combine speech recognition with text analysis. This demonstration shows two of those applications, Meeting-Miner and Data Broadcast. Although many problems remain, our preliminary results are encouraging. Many more details about the issues and systems described here and a rich bibliography can be found in [1].

References

[1] E. W. Brown, S. Srinivasan, A. Coden, D. Ponceleon, J. W. Cooper, and A. Amir. Toward speech as a knowledge resource. *IBM Systems Journal*, 40(4), 2001.
[2] A. Coden and E. Brown. Speech transcript analysis for automatic search. In *Proc. of HICSS-34*, Hawaii, 2001.
[3] J. Prager, E. Brown, A. Coden, and D. Radev. Question-answering by predictive annotation. In *Proc. of the 23rd Inter. ACM SIGIR Conf. On Res. And Develop. in Information Retrieval*, pages 184–191, Athens, Greece, 2000.

Author Index

Lecture Notes in Computer Science

For information about Vols. 1–2185
please contact your bookseller or Springer-Verlag

Vol. 2226: K.P. Jantke, A. Shinohara (Eds.), Discovery Science. Proceedings, 2001. XII, 494 pages. 2001. (Subseries LNAI).

Vol. 2227: S. Boztaş, I.E. Shparlinski (Eds.), Applied Algebra, Algebraic Algorithms and Error-Correcting Codes. Proceedings, 2001. XII, 398 pages. 2001.

Vol. 2228: B. Monien, V.K. Prasanna, S. Vajapeyam (Eds.), High Performance Computing – HiPC 2001. Proceedings, 2001. XVIII, 438 pages. 2001.

Vol. 2229: S. Qing, T. Okamoto, J. Zhou (Eds.), Information and Communications Security. Proceedings, 2001. XIV, 504 pages. 2001.

Vol. 2230: T. Katila, I.E. Magnin, P. Clarysse, J. Montagnat, J. Nenonen (Eds.), Functional Imaging and Modeling of the Heart. Proceedings, 2001. XI, 158 pages. 2001.

Vol. 2231: A. Pasetti, Software Frameworks and Embedded Control Systems. XIV, 293 pages. 2002.

Vol. 2232: L. Fiege, G. Mühl, U. Wilhelm (Eds.), Electronic Commerce. Proceedings, 2001. X, 233 pages. 2001.

Vol. 2233: J. Crowcroft, M. Hofmann (Eds.), Networked Group Communication. Proceedings, 2001. X, 205 pages. 2001.

Vol. 2234: L. Pacholski, P. Ružička (Eds.), SOFSEM 2001: Theory and Practice of Informatics. Proceedings, 2001. XI, 347 pages. 2001.

Vol. 2235: C.S. Calude, G. Păun, G. Rozenberg, A. Salomaa (Eds.), Multiset Processing. VIII, 359 pages. 2001.

Vol. 2236: K. Drira, A. Martelli, T. Villemur (Eds.), Co-operative Environments for Distributed Systems Engineering. IX, 281 pages. 2001.

Vol. 2237: P. Codognet (Ed.), Logic Programming. Proceedings, 2001. XI, 365 pages. 2001.

Vol. 2239: T. Walsh (Ed.), Principles and Practice of Constraint Programming – CP 2001. Proceedings, 2001. XIV, 788 pages. 2001.

Vol. 2240: G.P. Picco (Ed.), Mobile Agents. Proceedings, 2001. XIII, 277 pages. 2001.

Vol. 2241: M. Jünger, D. Naddef (Eds.), Computational Combinatorial Optimization. IX, 305 pages. 2001.

Vol. 2242: C.A. Lee (Ed.), Grid Computing – GRID 2001. Proceedings, 2001. XII, 185 pages. 2001.

Vol. 2243: G. Bertrand, A. Imiya, R. Klette (Eds.), Digital and Image Geometry. VII, 455 pages. 2001.

Vol. 2244: D. Bjørner, M. Broy, A.V. Zamulin (Eds.), Perspectives of System Informatics. Proceedings, 2001. XIII, 548 pages. 2001.

Vol. 2245: R. Hariharan, M. Mukund, V. Vinay (Eds.), FST TCS 2001: Foundations of Software Technology and Theoretical Computer Science. Proceedings, 2001. XI, 347 pages. 2001.

Vol. 2246: R. Falcone, M. Singh, Y.-H. Tan (Eds.), Trust in Cyber-societies. VIII, 195 pages. 2001. (Subseries LNAI).

Vol. 2247: C. P. Rangan, C. Ding (Eds.), Progress in Cryptology – INDOCRYPT 2001. Proceedings, 2001. XIII, 351 pages. 2001.

Vol. 2248: C. Boyd (Ed.), Advances in Cryptology – ASIACRYPT 2001. Proceedings, 2001. XI, 603 pages. 2001.

Vol. 2249: K. Nagi, Transactional Agents. XVI, 205 pages. 2001.

Vol. 2250: R. Nieuwenhuis, A. Voronkov (Eds.), Logic for Programming, Artificial Intelligence, and Reasoning. Proceedings, 2001. XV, 738 pages. 2001. (Subseries LNAI).

Vol. 2251: Y.Y. Tang, V. Wickerhauser, P.C. Yuen, C.Li (Eds.), Wavelet Analysis and Its Applications. Proceedings, 2001. XIII, 450 pages. 2001.

Vol. 2252: J. Liu, P.C. Yuen, C. Li, J. Ng, T. Ishida (Eds.), Active Media Technology. Proceedings, 2001. XII, 402 pages. 2001.

Vol. 2253: T. Terano, T. Nishida, A. Namatame, S. Tsumoto, Y. Ohsawa, T. Washio (Eds.), New Frontiers in Artificial Intelligence. Proceedings, 2001. XXVII, 553 pages. 2001. (Subseries LNAI).

Vol. 2254: M.R. Little, L. Nigay (Eds.), Engineering for Human-Computer Interaction. Proceedings, 2001. XI, 359 pages. 2001.

Vol. 2255: J. Dean, A. Gravel (Eds.), COTS-Based Software Systems. Proceedings, 2002. XIV, 257 pages. 2002.

Vol. 2256: M. Stumptner, D. Corbett, M. Brooks (Eds.), AI 2001: Advances in Artificial Intelligence. Proceedings, 2001. XII, 666 pages. 2001. (Subseries LNAI).

Vol. 2257: S. Krishnamurthi, C.R. Ramakrishnan (Eds.), Practical Aspects of Declarative Languages. Proceedings, 2002. VIII, 351 pages. 2002.

Vol. 2258: P. Brazdil, A. Jorge (Eds.), Progress in Artificial Intelligence. Proceedings, 2001. XII, 418 pages. 2001. (Subseries LNAI).

Vol. 2259: S. Vaudenay, A.M. Youssef (Eds.), Selected Areas in Cryptography. Proceedings, 2001. XI, 359 pages. 2001.

Vol. 2260: B. Honary (Ed.), Cryptography and Coding. Proceedings, 2001. IX, 416 pages. 2001.

Vol. 2262: P. Müller, Modular Specification and Verification of Object-Oriented Programs. XIV, 292 pages. 2002.

Vol. 2264: K. Steinhöfel (Ed.), Stochastic Algorithms: Foundations and Applications. Proceedings, 2001. VIII, 203 pages. 2001.

Vol. 2267: M. Cerioli, G. Reggio (Eds.), Recent Trends in Algebraic Development Techniques. Proceedings, 2001. X, 345 pages. 2001.

Vol. 2272: D. Bert, J.P. Bowen, M.C. Henson, K. Robinson (Eds.), ZB 2002: Formal Specification and Development in Z and B. Proceedings, 2002. XII, 535 pages. 2002.

Vol. 2273: A.R. Coden, E.W. Brown, S. Srinivasan (Eds.), Information Retrieval Techniques for Speech Applications. XI, 109 pages. 2002.

Vol. 2274: D. Naccache, P. Paillier (Eds.), Public Key Cryptography. Proceedings, 2002. XI, 385 pages. 2002.

Vol. 2275: N.R. Pal, M. Sugeno (Eds.), Advances in Soft Computing – AFSS 2002. Proceedings, 2002. XVI, 536 pages. 2002. (Subseries LNAI).